loved like jesus

VIKKI WATERS

Growing in Grace Ministries
423.605.2268
www.vikkiwaters.com
www.iggm.org

Editing: Amy Calkins | www.aurora-pub.com
Cover Design: © Yvonne Parks | www.pearcreative.ca
Interior Layout: © Renee Evans | www.reneeevansdesign.com
Banner by Freepik

ISBN 978-0-9966744-6-1

Printed in the United States of America

To my husband—you are my best friend and closest companion on the journey of experiencing the Father's love.

Endorsements

Every person who reads *Loved Like Jesus* will gain fresh insight into the love of the Father and our ability to be vessels of that love. With her unique and refreshing approach to the story of the prodigal son, Vikki communicates the importance of transitioning from a performance-oriented relationship with the Father to one of position—the position of a son or daughter. Living in a day when so many are plagued with an orphan spirit, she effectively shows the contrast between the older son's performance-based lifestyle and the extravagant love of the Father.

DR. TOM JONES
Executive Director
Global Awakening

You were made for love! Reading *Loved Like Jesus* stirred my heart to encounter more of this eternal love—God's love pouring in and then first-love passion pouring out. Vikki Waters' amazing book will bring you into the presence of the God of Love! Consider it a road map back into God's heart. You'll find yourself identifying with Vikki's journey and her message. Make sure you pick up a copy for a friend and your pastor. *Loved Like Jesus* will change your life!

DR. BRIAN SIMMONS
Stairway Ministries
The Passion Translation Project

Raw, honest, and profound, Vikki Waters' new book is fantastic! Taking you by the hand, she will guide you to a healthy heart, an open heart of love, and finally a heart in union with the presence of God.

DR. JONATHAN WELTON
Best-selling author
Founder of Welton Academy

I have known Vikki for many years, and she is the real, authentic deal. She possesses an uncommon mixture of passion and wisdom. You will find her insights and the way she portrays God's love refreshing and warming of the heart.

ANDY REESE
Director of The Freedom Resource

I am excited to endorse both this book and its author. Vikki is touching on a subject that the world needs to know and the Church needs to be re-introduced to. It is the final answer for what our hearts really long for on a daily basis. We were made to experience the Father's love. You will be truly blessed with her straightforward style as she leads you into His presence and teaches you how to dwell there. Enjoy!

JIM BANKS
Founder, Director
House of Healing Ministries and Traumaprayer.com

Acknowledgements

Writing a book takes a team of people!

Thank you to the faith-filled people who have come alongside me and pointed me toward Jesus and my Father's love. I have finally discovered how to be a good receiver of His love and give it away to others.

Thank you, also, to the many risk-takers who have stepped out of their comfort zone and pursued healing through Growing in Grace Ministries. Your courage and quest for our Father's true heart is such an encouragement. Watching you walk out your healing and helping others do the same builds my faith. I remain your biggest cheerleader and fan!

Thank you to my Growing in Grace Ministries team! We are truly family. Doing life with you is the greatest joy and privilege. You are the real deal. Thank you for the sacrifices you make every week to minister to the broken. My ceiling is your floor, and you astonish me season after season. You are champions of creating a safe place to encounter His presence and experience lasting breakthrough. Papa is incredibly proud of how you represent Him!

Amy Calkins, thank you for your brilliant editing and for helping me take this message to the next level. I'm forever grateful.

Yvonne Parks and Renee Evans, thank you for your excellence and creativity in design from cover to cover.

To my Growing in Grace Ministries church family and online students, thank you for showing up week after week to hear me teach about the goodness of our Father, Jesus, and Holy Spirit. You are a vital part of our mandate to equip sons and daughters for abundant living, lasting freedom, and effective ministry.

Finally, to those who are reading this book, thank you for embracing the journey you are about to step into. You won't be the same! Get ready for a very real and tangible deepening of your relationship with the one who is absolutely crazy about you. I appreciate the time you are investing in searching for the *more* of God. He will not disappoint you!

Contents

Introduction

In 1991, at the age of twenty-six, I was ambitiously climbing the corporate ladder as fast as I could. As a young mother, an energetic entrepreneur, and an all around over-achiever in my community and church, I believed my driven personality was serving me well.

Then, in the summer of that year, I was invited to attend a seventy-two-hour spiritual retreat. *Oh great*, I thought, *I need some rest!* On that weekend, much to my surprise, I met the author of rest—Jesus—for the first time. He wooed my often hard and distant heart with demonstrations of His *unconditional love*. During the retreat, people I had never before met loved me extravagantly—graciously serving me, singing and praying over me, and deeply encouraging me. Through them, I tangibly saw and experienced the goodness of God, and as a result, I decided to surrender my life to Him.

This decision to invite Jesus into my life changed everything—especially for my family. Prior to the retreat, my husband, Richard, and I had been experiencing serious marital issues. We had been on the brink of divorce more than once. But, my encounter with Jesus had changed me. When I came home from the retreat, it didn't take Richard long to realize something big had happened in my heart. Because of this, he began to seek after what I had experienced and eventually also gave His heart to God.

In the wake of my God encounter, like most new Christians, I began enthusiastically getting to know Jesus. Over the next eleven years, I diligently sought Him with passion and dedication. As a result, I was growing and experiencing positive change in myself and my relationships. Yet, for the most part, I was still in the driver's seat of my life. Jesus was my Savior, but I had not fully surrendered to the transforming work of His Holy Spirit. Instead, I focused my energy on serving and "getting things done" for the Kingdom. I knew something was missing, and I was totally exhausted. I wanted *more*, but I did not know what that more was.

Then, one day while I was studying the Book of Revelation, God showed me something I had never seen before. He opened my eyes to a truth that would change my life. In Revelation 2:2, Jesus says to the church in Ephesus, *"I know your deeds, your hard work and your perseverance."* These things are all commendable. But Jesus continues, *"Yet I hold this against you: you have forsaken the love you had at first"* (Rev. 2:4). I'd read this passage many times over the years, and I thought I knew what Jesus meant by *"first love."* But as I mulled over those familiar words, Jesus began to show me something deeper. He whispered to me that, though I had the deeds, hard work, and perseverance down pat, I still needed to experience that *first love*.

As I prayed over and meditated on this verse, the Holy Spirit showed me what I had been missing. He pointed me back toward the Father, who was inviting me into a special relationship with Him. See, the problem that Jesus came to fix was the broken relationship between God and His children. Humanity had wondered far from His heart, and Jesus came to free us from the oppression of sin and death so that we could be reunited with our Father. He also restored our rightful identity as the children of God. The point was never what I could accomplish for God or how well I could perform on my own strength.

When I'd accepted Jesus into my heart, I'd allowed my driven personality and my wounds from the past to inform my faith, and I became a works-oriented Christian. Somehow, though I'd been wooed by God's unconditional love, once I was in His Kingdom, I was driven by performance, not by love. This, I was discovering, was contrary to what the gospel was all about. Jesus had come as an exact representation of the Father's heart toward me. He had come because of love. He had come because *He is love*. The Holy Spirit showed me this reality in First John, where it says: *"And so we know and rely on the love God has for us. God is love. Whoever lives in love lives in God, and God in them....We love because he first loved us"* (1 John 4:16, 19).

The Living Bible translates these verses a little differently:

*We know how much God loves us because we have felt His love and because we believe Him when He tells us that He loves us dearly. God is love, and anyone who lives in love is living with God and God is living in him....So you see our love for Him comes as a result of **His loving us first.***

In other words, the *first love* is the love of God the Father for us. This revelation changed me. For years, I had known in my head that God loves me. But now, for the first time, I realized I could personally experience the love of my heavenly Father in my heart! I did not have to perform to obtain His love; I already had access to His heart simply because He had given it to me. God had loved me first—before I knew His name, before I had done any good works for Him—and nothing I could do would change that.

This realization put the previous years of my life in Christ into a new light. Suddenly I realized I'd been striving and working hard for something I already had. No wonder I was exhausted and discontented. I had gotten it all backward, thinking I had to earn Father God's love.

Instead, the truth was, He already loved me—eternally and unconditionally. Not only that, but His love in my heart was the catalyst that would help me love Him back. In this way, I would be able to truly and freely love and serve God—not out of duty or performance but because of love. This is exactly what Jesus modeled in His life on earth. As a human, He experienced the Father's love for Him, and that love enabled everything Jesus did. We, too, are made to experience God's love in the same way that Jesus did, and as a result, to live as empowered sons and daughters of God.

That's what this book is all about—experiencing God's love for us as His children and, from that place of love, learning to walk in confidence and power. We will discover what God's love is really like, how to live in our identity and inheritance as His children, how to overcome in the midst of trials, and how to live from a place of rest. All this is rooted in the revelation of the *first love* that God has for us—the *same love* that He has for Jesus (see John 17:23).

My prayer is that, like me, you will begin to experience the joy of a deep love relationship with Papa God. To help you along this journey of discovery, at the end of each chapter I've inserted a "Getting Personal" section with questions and activities designed to help you make these revelations personal in your own life. I bless you on your journey!

CHAPTER 1

Sons and Daughters

Not long ago, I learned that when I was a baby, one of my primary caregivers regularly told me that my mother didn't love me and that's why she left me to go to work every day. Of course, when this was discovered, my parents found a new babysitter, but the invisible damage had already been done. Although I was too young to understand the words spoken over me, my little heart somehow experienced the power of the lies. As I grew older, the fruit of this was a painful longing to be loved, which began to show up in my thoughts about myself, my expectations of those close to me, and my self-protective behavior. Deep down in my heart, I believed there was something fatally wrong with me. This lie facilitated an explosive and destructive self-hatred, as I aimlessly searched for relief and love in all the wrong places. Even when I accepted Jesus into my life, my inner pain kept me from engaging with God's heart from me. Though I intellectually knew He loved me, my own wounds kept me for experiencing His love in a way that would heal and transform my heart.

My story is not unique. Though the reasons behind our pain are varied, this reality is common to many Christians. Like me, they have not experienced the *first love* of God for them, and as a result, they do not know who they really are. Jesus told a story about a son like this—two sons in fact. Neither knew their father's heart toward them. Though one turned to wild living and the other to performance, their need was the same: a revelation of the unconditional love of their father.

A relook at this well-worn story of two sons and their father (see Luke 15) is a first step on our journey toward knowing God's love and who we are in light of His love. Most Christians have heard this story more times than they can count. Perhaps that's because it contains one of the Bible's most compelling analogies of Father God's love for us.

Many Bibles refer to this story as the parable of the prodigal son. I like to refer to the father, not the younger son, in this story as the true prodigal, because the word *prodigal*, according to the *Merriam-Webster Dictionary*, means "one who spends or gives lavishly and foolishly." It is true that the first son spent his inheritance prodigally—he *"squandered his wealth in wild living"* (Luke 15:13). However, his actions pale in comparison to the prodigal nature of the father's response to his son. It is the father—whose lavish and foolish demonstrations of love defy reason and responsibility—who is the greatest prodigal of this story. And his prodigal love gives us a picture of the reckless, extravagant, and unreasonable love of Father God for us.

This is God's heart for all of His sons and daughters, for every person ever born. He is extreme, excessive, and extravagant with His love toward His children, even when those children have wandered far from His heart. In Jesus' parable, we see in both sons a picture of God's response to those children who have wandered from His heart.

THE FIELDS OF INDEPENDENCE

First, Jesus tells of the younger son, who asked for his inheritance early and then wasted it in wild living far from home. This son, discontented with His father's love and home, left in search of his identity in the fields of independence.

After the son left his father's home, three events happened in rapid succession. First, he wasted his entire inheritance on wild living. Second, a severe famine hit the land. Third, he ended up in great need. Bankrupted financially, morally, and spiritually, he needed immediate help. But his physical poverty was only the surface of his problem. Beneath that lived a heartbreak and despair too deep for words. Because of his need for food, the son took a job with a pig farmer despite the fact that his religion taught that pigs are unclean. For him, this must have been terribly humiliating. It would have been difficult for him to sink much lower. The quickness with which this young man sank should not surprise us. It is the way of sin. When we look for significance and satisfaction in the world, we will end up in bondage, reaping the consequences of our poor choices. Sin always takes us farther than we meant to go. That's exactly what happened to this young man.

He became so desperately hungry that he longed to eat the pig's food, but he had nothing. All of the friends who had encouraged him in his wild living had abandoned him in his trouble. This is the strategy of the enemy of our souls. He leads us astray with counterfeit dreams and then laughs at us when we land in the pig pen, leaving us alone in our misery. This was the sorry end of the son's venture into the fields of independence.

Knowing that he came from a wealthy, godly, and loving home, we might wonder what could have driven him to make such poor decisions. Why was he so dissatisfied with all he had? What caused him to desert his upbringing and his loving father? While Jesus does not say what caused this younger son to act as he did, we know he is a picture of what happens when people wander from God. The consequences of his wild living show us how messy life without God at the center can be. That is certainly the plight of the lost person, though not always in such extreme ways. But the younger son is also a picture of those who have experienced the love and provision of God and yet have concluded it wasn't enough. As a result, they went searching for greener pastures.

GREENER PASTURES

These greener pastures are, of course, an illusion—one that can cause us to become dissatisfied with God's abundant provision and loving embrace. The NIV uses the term *wild living* to describe the son's search for greener pastures. It could also be termed *addictive living*. It is the way people self-medicate their pain through escape, excess, and addiction in various forms, including food, sex, television, sleep, spending, work, alcohol and drugs, exercise, pornography, activity, relationships, social media, video games, gambling, and so forth.

To the son, the wild, addictive life seemed greener. It seemed somehow better and more exciting. For this reason, he left the security and safety of his father's house. Like him, many of us are attracted to and easily fall into self-destructive behaviors, which entice us despite our past experiences of God's love. Most often, the reason we are fooled by the illusion of the greener pasture is rooted in one of two heart problems.

The first problem is *unhealed pain in our hearts*. When we are wounded, it's like a little place in our souls is broken or crushed. The more pain we experience, the more broken our hearts become. Since this process begins in our very early years, many of us grow up accumulating a lot of pain at the hands of others, our environment, our circumstances, and our own self-sabotage. To try to make the pain stop, we self-medicate through addictive living. As a result, we end up in terrible bondage, wondering how to end the constant turmoil in our hearts. Only Jesus can heal the pain in our hearts. He is the one who came to bind up the brokenhearted (see Isa. 61:1); it's His specialty. But instead of turning to Jesus for healing, many people try everything else. In my own life, I spent many wasted years self-medicating for a variety of reasons. Here are at least three:

1. I was afraid of being vulnerable because I didn't know how to trust others with my heart. The unhealed filter of my past experiences taught me that the risk of trust would likely result in more injury through judgment, betrayal, and wounding.

2. At times, my pain was so familiar to me that I couldn't imagine life without it. Even though it wasn't helping or working for me, it was what I knew.

3. At other times, I feared being rejected and thought if people knew the real me or things from my past they would not like me. All this resulted in me rejecting most people before they had a chance to reject me.

Because of these reasons and more, many who seek greener pastures must come to the end of themselves, like the younger son, before they will return to the Father.

The second problem is an *unmet core need for love*. This may seem like a contradiction. How could a person experience the unconditional love of the Father, yet still have an unmet core need for love? The answer is simple. If we do not believe God loved us first, we will struggle to experience the love He feels toward us. We are all born with a place in our hearts designed to receive and be filled to overflowing with the love of God. But until we learn how to have a genuine relationship with Him, our longing for love will be unsatisfied, and we will try desperately to fill the void on our own.

When we receive Christ in our hearts and are born again into our new nature, we are supernaturally transferred from the kingdom of darkness into the Kingdom and family of God. Satan no longer controls us (see Col. 1:9–14). We become citizens and inheritors of that Kingdom, and we have access to all the blessings and security of that Kingdom. Jesus wants to heal our hearts completely and fully meet our core need for love so that we can discover who we are in Him and live as fully free and mature children of God. But we always have a choice. Time and time again people try to meet their own needs because at some point in their lives they had legitimate needs that somehow went unmet. For instance, as children we all have the need for provision, security, safety, companionship, nurturing, instruction, and comfort in our family relationships. If any of these needs are not met, we develop a belief that we need to take on the responsibility to meet our own needs in those areas. This causes a big problem in our relationship with Father God, Jesus, and Holy Spirit, as well as in our earthly relationships. When this is the case, we have a choice about whether we turn to Him to meet our needs or remain stuck in a cycle of lack. Many Christians allow the pain of their past to put a limit on their relationship with God.

Because of this, they are susceptible to the enemy's lies. The enemy cannot snatch us from our Father (see John 10:27–30), but he can lie to us about who we are and what will satisfy our hearts. He tries to persuade us to wander from our Father and live as though we are still citizens of darkness. He promises that the excesses and addictions of the wild life will meet our heart cry. When we listen to his voice, we empower his lies in our lives. We make ourselves vulnerable to his attack. This is exactly what happened to the younger son. When he left home to pursue greener pastures, he became vulnerable, and the enemy brought famine and poverty into his life.

This was the choice the son made. When we listen to the enemy's lies and pursue satisfaction in the wild life, we too are making a choice. The enemy cannot force us to believe his lies. The son did not need to go, and neither do we. Often, if we believe we are unloved and our hearts are full of pain, it is easy to blame our circumstances on others. The truth is, when we are tempted, we always have a way of escape. The apostle Paul made this clear:

No temptation has overtaken you except what is common to mankind. And God is faithful; he will not let you be tempted beyond what you can bear. But when you are tempted, he will also provide a way out so that you can endure it (1 Corinthians 10:13).

We can always choose to stay close to the Father's heart, wrapped in His protective embrace and trusting His healing work in our lives. All we have to do is turn to the Holy Spirit. If we are willing, He will help us recognize the truth and make good choices.

When we chose, instead, to wander from God's heart, it becomes harder and harder for us to recognize the truth about God and about ourselves. Our minds are flooded with lies, and we begin to hate ourselves, imagining that our Father also hates us. Yet, the Father always holds open a door of escape. No matter what we may do, that door remains open to us. That door, as it was for the son, is simply an invitation to return home to the Father.

COMING HOME

In Jesus' parable, the younger son finally comes to his senses and decides to stop acting like an orphan and humbly return to his father (see Luke 15:18). The fact that it took him so long to remember the love of his father shows us that the son was an orphan at heart, even though he had a good father. This false orphan identity in his heart caused him to question his father's love for him, so that even as he was returning, he devised a plan for how to convince his father to let him stay—not as a son but as a servant. Whether we realize it or not, many of us, like the younger son, view ourselves as orphans who are unworthy of God's love. As a result, we have a hard time receiving it. I realized this in my own life when my dad gave me a beautiful watch he'd found at a thrift store. I could immediately tell it was worth quite a bit, and my first response was, "Oh my goodness! How extravagant! You shouldn't give this to me; you could sell it and make money on this find." My dad just smiled at me.

Then I heard Father God gently say, "This is your perspective on My gifts sometimes, too. Sometimes you point out how you don't deserve My lavish gifts, but you need to realize that when I look at you, I see Jesus. Therefore, you are always worthy of My best gifts. I give My kids only good gifts out of the treasure of My heart and Kingdom (see Matt. 7:11; Luke 12:32). Receive this with great joy!" Immediately, I changed my tune and thanked my dad for his gift, giving him a big hug. Now, when I look at my watch, I am reminded of the way Father God reaches toward me and engulfs me in His lavish love. This revelation is so important to our identity as children of God. If we don't understand that we are loveable and worthy of His best gifts, we will be prone to wandering.

When God's children stray from His heart, it is often because they, too, wrongly see themselves as unlovable orphans. This causes them to question the Father's love for them, no matter what He does. It causes them to expect, like the younger son, that they will not be welcomed home as children, but only as servants. Of course, the father's prodigal response to his son's return is the opposite of all he had expected. Jesus tells us the father saw his son coming, even when he was still far away (see Luke 15:20). That means he was daily waiting and looking for his son to return home. At first sight of him, the father ran to meet his son, embraced him, and kissed him, even before the son was able to voice his apology. Quickly, the father demonstrated his forgiveness and acceptance, welcoming the son back as his *son* (not servant) and showering him with extravagant and undeserved gifts (see Luke 15:20–24).

Though the son was dirty, the father put a bright new robe on him—a special garment signifying his belonging within the family. The father also put a signet ring on the son's finger; this ring would have been the son's proof of his identity as the son of his father. Finally, the father gave his son shoes. In that day, servants did not wear shoes, and the son had most likely returned barefooted. In answer to the son's suggestion that he could be a servant in his father's house, the father gave him new shoes, placing him above the servants and making him an heir in the family business. In this way, the father demonstrated that he was fully restoring the son to his identity as a son and to his relationship with the father.

This is exactly how our heavenly Father responds to us when we stray from His heart and then find our way back home. He does not scold or punish or make us prove we have changed. He does not take away our status as His children and heirs in His Kingdom. Instead, He welcomes us home with open arms, rejoicing in our return. And like the father in the story, He reminds us of our inheritance as His children. He gives us the robe of righteousness, which shows our right standing with the Father and membership in the royal family. He marks and seals us with His Spirit, who reminds us of our true identity as sons and daughters. And He gives us the shoes of peace, with authority to co-labor in the family business to establish His Kingdom wherever the soles of our feet tread. This is the Father's heart toward us.

We did nothing to earn salvation; we simply accepted His free gift of relationship, through Jesus' redemptive work on the cross. Of the Father's love, John says: *"See what great love the Father has lavished on us, that we should be called children of God! And that is what we are"* (1 John 3:1). His love for us is not simply love, but lavish love—love in abundance and excess. In His great generosity,

God does not just love us, but He adopts us as His children. We do nothing to earn our place in His hearts, and we do not need to do anything to earn our way back into His heart. Instead, He always holds us in His heart, even when we chose to walk away from Him and make choices that hurt Him. As the best Father there is, He never stops loving us. In fact, Paul says nothing can separate us from God's love for us (see Rom. 8:35–39). The only thing that can come between us and the Father's love is our own choice to walk away. And even then, His love remains, always available and awaiting our return.

This is God's heart toward all His children, whether we stray from Him or not. It is His heart toward those who, like the other brother in this story, have not strayed into wild living but who have tried to earn the Father's love through performance.

THE FIELDS OF PERFORMANCE

Many of us, at times, have wandered from the Father's heart and lived like orphans in the fields of independence. Many more of us have stayed closer to home, but we have sought for significance and approval in the fields of performance. This happens when we allow a performance-oriented mindset to dominate our relationship with God, and we begin to believe we are loved only when we perform well. This also is orphan-hearted thinking. In a healthy family relationship, children never need to earn their parents' love or their identity in the family.

Yet, unfortunately, many of us learned this kind of thinking as children. If we behaved well, we were rewarded. If we didn't, we were punished. Even if it was unintentional, the way our parents delivered those rewards and punishments left us believing that their love and approval depended on how we performed. Children who learn to perform for love often grow into adults who think they need to earn love from other people and even from God. This mindset can manifest in a variety of behaviors that look good on the outside, but the heart motivation is rooted in insecurity and an orphan heart.

Performance is the route the older brother in Jesus' story chose. Though like his younger brother he had experienced the love and provision of his father, he came to believe he had earned that love through good behavior and must continue to do so (see Luke 15:25–32). Because of this mindset, when his younger brother returned home, the older brother resented his father's response, and he refused to join in the celebration. Here we see a sharp contrast between the father and the older son. The father forgave because his love for his son was not based upon his son's behavior. The older son refused to forgive because he was bitter about what he saw as injustice: His brother did not receive punishment for his poor choices but instead was celebrated. It seemed unfair to him, because he was out of touch with the father's heart and focused, instead, on all he was doing for the father.

A FAULTY MINDSET

This faulty mindset led the older son to completely miss out on the father's heart. In the face of this incredible demonstration of the father's love, the older son argued that his own behavior had been consistently good, especially compared to that of his brother. In other words, the older son felt his father's love for him should have been greater than the love he felt for the younger son, because the older son's behavior had been better. He believed love and acceptance are based on performance rather than relationship and identity. Because of this, the older son's resentment and offense effectively rendered him just as lost from his father's love as his younger brother had been. This is Jesus' point—the prodigal father had two very different sons with equally incorrect perspectives on their relationship with him. Both had wandered from his love. Their ungodly beliefs, judgments, and perceptions had intensified their dissatisfaction, making them blind to their father's love for them.

When we adopt a performance-based mindset, we welcome shame and fear into our lives. Shame tells us something is wrong with us. Fear tells us we will be rejected, we don't belong, and we won't measure up. The result is control. Without realizing it, we begin to overcompensate by trying to exert control. Control tells us to strive to win the approval of others. Then we will feel better about ourselves, be accepted, and fill our love void. But it is a lie, a very futile and exhausting lie.

Like many of us, I spent years striving for love and approval because of this mindset. When I first met Christ in my late twenties, I had been wandering in the fields of independence for years, determined to do it my way. When I finally came home to God, instead of getting to know the heart of my extravagant Father, I went directly into the fields of performance and began searching for something I already had access to.

Well-meaning friends and church members saw my enthusiasm and energy for serving the Lord. They quickly began giving me advice about things to do and activities to get involved in. Being young in the Lord and perhaps a little naïve, I thought that was what a new Christian was supposed to do. So, for the first few years of my Christian life I continued to busy myself in one ministry activity after another. What I did not realize was that I had a lot of unhealed pain in my heart. My default mode, when I had lived in independence, was to cope with my pain through busyness, serving, and performing for significance. As long as I was on the go, I could keep a lid on my heart issues, and no one would know how miserable I really was. This mindset transferred into my life with God, and instead of allowing Him to heal my heart, I self-medicated the pain through good Christian service.

This pace went on for a number of years. I juggled a full-time career and volunteered several hours a week, serving in the church in various positions and committees. Then, in 1996, I left my successful career and plunged into two demanding ministry roles. I became the part-time director of a start-up ministry to Christian business women, and I also began an intense pastoral training program as a chaplain at our local trauma center hospital. The latter position kept me in fight-or-flight mode on a daily basis. My duties required me to regularly face death, tragedy, and the fragility of human life for almost a year. Still masking the pain, I had convinced myself I had it all under control.

Then one day everything fell apart. I could no longer contain everything I had bottled up and stuffed down over the years. I became deeply offended at two of my Christian colleagues. It seems very silly now, but at the time, because of my deep inner wounds, it was devastating. I felt rejected by something they had done at a conference we were involved with. Their actions touched the ungodly belief I harbored—*Something is wrong with me.* I began to build a case against them in my mind. *I have worked so hard to measure up, and I deserve their approval!* The more I stewed over the offense, the angrier I became. In the end, I stormed away from this event, where I had responsibilities. Of course, my two friends had not done anything to intentionally hurt me. But in my mind, their actions seemed very personal and pointed. They had pressed an invisible button deep within my heart, and all the pain that had been repressed for such a long time came spewing out. It was incredibly ugly.

The result was an unveiling of the true condition of my heart. All the pain that had surfaced could no longer be ignored. I needed help and healing for my heart. Because I did not know how to find what I needed, I slipped into a period of deep depression. I could not even pretend to perform. I had come to the end of myself. Years of ministry to others had not healed me. Seminary and ordination had not healed me. Leading others had not healed me. I had been looking in the wrong place, in the field of performance. Thankfully, I met some people who helped me deal with my baggage and introduced me to the healing power of God's Spirit. With their guidance, I invited Him to bind up the broken places in my heart, and over a period of time, He did just that. Other believers also came alongside me and supported me in my restoration journey.

One time, one of these people prayed for me, asking God to show me a time when I had felt unloved and alone. The first thing that came to my mind was a memory from when I was very little. I saw myself sitting in a corner crying. Then, in my mind's eye, I saw Jesus there with me, wrapping me in His strong arms and holding me tight. In that moment, for the first time in my life, I actually experienced the unseen arms of God, and I was forever changed. I discovered the truth about my real identity. That day, I heard Him whisper to me, "You are dearly loved, cherished, and adored. I delight in you every day. I created you to be loved and to rest in My embrace." And He asked me, "Would you like to give Me the old lies in exchange for these life-giving truths?" I said yes, of course. That day, the Holy Spirit renewed my mind to those truths and filled me with a deep confidence in my Father's love.

This experience changed my life. Finally, I had found my Father's heart. Finally, I realized I did not need to do anything to earn or keep His love. In fact, He began to show me that my previous performance mindset was contrary to relationship with Him and had kept me from experiencing the love He wanted to give me. By contrast, as I learned to receive His love as a gift, I discovered that His love in me overflowed out of me and enabled me to genuinely love and serve others. I learned I could only love others *to the degree that I was willing to experience His love for me*. No longer was I serving to earn love; I was serving from an overflow of love. This heart healing and transformation profoundly impacted my life. In the wake of learning how to be loved and to love, God gave me a new vision for my life.

IDENTIFYING THE SYMPTOMS

Like me, many believers have spent years in performance, trying to earn the love God has freely given them. They have become like the older brother. Because this mindset is often learned in childhood, it can be difficult for us to identify what is really going on in our hearts. Our actions look great, but beneath the surface, our wounds are festering. I had to come to the end of myself before I was willing to really look deeply at why I was acting the way I was. Through my healing process, I discovered some of the predominate symptoms of the performance mindset. Recognizing them can help us avoid wandering from our Father's heart.

1. Striving

In His story, Jesus tells us that the older brother was in the field, away from home. Although the Scripture does not explicitly say it, the picture we get is of a workaholic. This is confirmed by the son's boasting about how hard he has worked for the father. We know we have fallen into the trap of performing when we find ourselves *striving or laboring* in ministry activities and at work without proper boundaries or rest. When we get to the point where we are consumed by these activities, we have probably wandered into the fields of performance.

2. Isolation

The older brother had also isolated himself from the family by working so hard in the fields. When he came to the house, he had to ask a servant what was going on. But by that time, he was already in a huff. There he was, working hard out in the field while other people were in the house feasting, dancing, and having a good time. Didn't they know there was work to be done? Didn't they know how unfair it was for him to be doing the father's work all by himself while they were in the house celebrating? Rather than go inside and investigate, he called for a servant to explain the situation. In so doing, he chose to further withdraw himself.

A sad byproduct of performance orientation is that we often end up isolating ourselves from the body of Christ. We frequently become perfectionists and convince ourselves that we are the only ones who can really perform a particular task well. We set out to do things by ourselves, looking at the faults and shortcomings of others we deem unable to perform as well as we can. This leads to an arrogant and short-tempered attitude that causes us to cut ourselves off from others.

3. Offended

When we are performance-oriented, we can also become *easily* offended by others. The older brother became angry when he discovered that his younger brother, who had not performed as well as he had, was the center of everyone's attention. This triggered the deep longing for love in the older brother's heart, and he became offended. He was resentful and bitter because he had not been recognized and appreciated. He felt the father had been holding out on him. As the older brother demonstrates, people with the performance mindset depend heavily on affirmation for their self-worth and value. When they come across people who are enjoying favor apart from behaving well, they become offended and angry.

4. Accusing

The older brother also accused his brother of behaving badly, and he even accused his father of inappropriately forgiving and rewarding the younger son. His thinking had become so self-centered and strict that he seemed incapable of feeling compassion for his younger brother or relief that he was safely home. Instead, he angrily accused him in an attempt to tear his brother down in the eyes of the father (and probably to make himself feel better).

When the performance mindset dominates our thinking and relationship with God, our thoughts toward others often become poisoned. Rules and accomplishments are the standards we use to measure others, leaving little room for forgiveness and grace. This is a depressing and lonely way to live. It causes broken relationships, ineffective ministry, and a deep sense of dissatisfaction. It also damages our relationship with our Heavenly Father—the very thing we thought we were strengthening through our obsession with performing for Him.

5. Pride

In the end, the older son's pride kept him from experiencing his father's love. He was so convinced that he was right in his offense that he could not see or receive the genuine love his father had for him. Jesus' parable ends with a picture of the son choosing to be stubborn and unforgiving. Nothing in the story suggests that the father got through to him; nothing indicates that his heart may have softened toward his brother. Instead, because of his offense, he refused to fellowship with the father, the younger brother, and the entire household. While everyone else celebrated, the older brother stayed outside. Even though he had a loving father, he chose to make himself an orphan in heart.

NO LONGER AN ORPHAN

In the story of the two sons, we see God's value for relationship over performance. That, of course, does not mean service to God isn't important. Serving is part of loving. But the bottom line is this: Our Heavenly Father does not base His love for us on what we do for Him. He does not love us more when we perform well, and He does not love us less when we fail. Instead, He loves us unconditionally, simply because we are His children. As a mother, though I am imperfect, I have a deep love for my daughter that transcends logic or explanation. She is always in my heart and on my mind. She always belongs with me and is valuable to me. This is an imperfect image of how much Father God thinks about us. We are always on His mind, not because He wants to control us but because He wants intimate relationship with us.

God is truly a prodigal Father, extravagant and reckless in His love for us. Knowing this and allowing ourselves to receive His love is the foundation of relationship with Him. Instead of searching for significance and approval in the fields of independence and performance, may we enter our Father's house and heart. There we will find the healing we need, the love our hearts have longed for.

Truth Declarations

I AM FULLY FORGIVEN BY GOD!

The Father has forgiven all my sins and remembers them no more (see Jer. 31:34).

He has put all my sins under His feet and has cast them into the depths of the sea (see Micah 7:19).

Through my relationship with Jesus, God is not counting my sins against me (see 2 Cor. 5:19).

I AM ALWAYS ACCEPTED BY GOD!

I am a child of God. I belong in His family (see John 1:12).

Jesus calls me His friend (see John 15:15).

In Christ, it is as if I had never sinned (see Rom. 5:1).

I belong to the Father and am a temple of the Holy Spirit (see 1 Cor. 6:19).

The Father knew and loved me before I was conceived (see Jer. 1:4–5).

I AM PLEASING IN THE FATHER'S EYE!

Even when I am wounded, the Father sees me as beautiful and takes great pleasure in me (see Ps. 149:4).

The Father's happy thoughts toward me are always filled with hope (see Jer. 29:11).

The Father is pleased that I am His child. He will never leave me and will meet all my needs (see Luke 15:31).

The Father likes being with me so much that He made His home within me (see John 14:23).

GETTING PERSONAL

1. Which of the two sons in Jesus' story do you identify with most? Why?

_____

_____

_____

_____

2. Have there been times in your life when you went searching in fields of independence? Are you there now? If so, are you willing to give your dissatisfaction and self-sufficiency to God? Pray something like this:

"Father, please forgive me for the ways I have tried to meet my own needs by _____ (be specific). I choose to turn away from those things and return to You. I give You my heartache and pain, trusting You to heal my heart. Come and fill me now with Your love and power. What would You like to give me in exchange?"

Write God's answer to you on the next page.

_____

_____

_____

_____

3. Consider the picture of God you have in your mind. How do you view Him as a result of this story? Is it different from how you viewed Him before?

_____

_____

_____

_____

4. Review the symptoms of performance orientation listed in the chapter. How many of them are evident in your life right now and to what degree?

_____

_____

_____

_____

5. Have there been times in your life when you were searching in fields of performance? Are you there now? If so, are you willing to give your striving and performing to God? Pray something like this:

_"Father, please forgive me for living with a performance mindset: _____ (be specific). I choose to give You all the striving and performing. Come and fill me now with Your love and power. What would You like to give me in exchange?"_ Write God's answer to you on the next page.

_____

_____

_____

_____

6. Using the Truth Declarations above, meditate on what Father God really thinks about you. Look up these truths one by one in your Bible and dialogue with the Lord by asking, *"Father, what do You want to say to me about this truth?"*

_____

_____

_____

_____

CHAPTER 2

Unseen Arms

Jesus, the author of the story of the two sons and their prodigal father, understands better than any of us the depths of the Father's love. After all, as the firstborn Son, Jesus was the first human to fully live in the Father's embrace. His experience opened the door for the rest of us to enjoy a close and loving relationship with our Father (see Rom. 8:29). To see the Father accurately, then, we must see Him as Jesus did during His life on earth.

In Matthew 3 we find perhaps the clearest picture of Jesus' personal experience of the Father's love. At the start of His public ministry, Jesus went to the Jordan River and asked John the Baptist to baptize Him. Matthew records the story this way:

As soon as Jesus was baptized, he went up out of the water. At that moment heaven was opened, and he saw the Spirit of God descending like a dove and alighting on him. And a voice from heaven said, "This is my Son, whom I love; with him I am well pleased" (Matthew 3:16–17).

In this simple event, Jesus was embraced by the unseen arms of the Father in two significant ways. This embrace confirmed His *identity* and filled Him with *power*, enabling Him to accomplish His life purpose.

This was necessary because, although He was fully God, Jesus was also fully human. When Jesus came to earth, He voluntarily left behind the attributes of His divinity in order to put on human flesh (see Phil. 2:5–8). Jesus had a human body just like ours, and He experienced the same kinds of practical needs and challenges we do—including hunger, thirst, exhaustion, and pain. He also had the full array of human emotions. Joy and sorrow, compassion and anger, peace and distress—Jesus had to deal with it all just like we do. And just like the rest of us, Jesus was wired with a core need for love that could only be fulfilled by His Father. This is exactly why Jesus needed to be baptized. Though He was perfect, He was also human, and He needed to begin His ministry with a reaffirmation of His Father's love. For this reason, when Jesus came up out of the water, God gave Him two signs of His love. The dove of the Spirit landed on Him, and God audibly declared Christ's identity as His loved and approved Son.

LOVED AND APPROVED

Jesus, like the rest of us, needed love and approval from His Father; He needed to know who He was as the Son. In other words, He needed to understand His identity. The Bible doesn't tell us how much Jesus knew about Himself from childhood, but somewhere along the way, He began to realize who He was and the special call on His life as the Messiah. Now, as a thirty-year-old man, ready to begin His public ministry, which would end on a cross, Jesus needed to be publicly affirmed in His identity. Thus, as John baptized Him, symbolically commissioning Him for His ministry, *"A voice from Heaven said, 'This is my son whom I love. With him I am well pleased'"* (Matt. 3:17). Here, the Father spoke to His Son's heart the two most important identity messages: love and approval.

In the original language, the Greek word *agapetos*, translated in the NIV as "loved," is more accurately translated "beloved."[1] In other words, the Father declared, *"This is My Son, My Beloved."* The Greek definition reveals the weight of this carefully chosen word, which would have communicated something like, "Son, I love You dearly; I adore You; I love You as My favorite!" It was as if Father God was wrapping Jesus tightly in His unseen arms. That's the emotional intensity portrayed in this scene.

This is what Jesus meant to the Father, and it is what we mean to Him, too. He has such love and value for each one of us that He views each one of us as though we were His favorite. By definition, *favorite* implies that only one person can hold that title. And the Bible makes is clear that God does not show favoritism (see Rom. 2:11). We are all equal before Him. But in our equality, we are each specially loved and adored as though we were His favorite. He gives us what we might call "favorite love."

When my daughter was younger, I would often pick her up, squeeze her tightly, and say, "You're my favorite!"

She would laugh, roll her eyes, and say, "Mom, I'm your *only* child."

"Yes," I would say, "but I love you as my favorite."

That is what Papa God says over each one of His children. He loves us like we are each His favorite. This same term, *beloved*, that God used for Jesus here is used sixty-one other places in the New Testament, often in reference to us, God's other children. In the same way that Jesus was loved, we are dearly loved, adored, and

---

[1] *Strong's Concordance*, Greek #27.

highly esteemed. *We* are each the beloved of God. Understanding the Father's love for us is the foundation of our identity as children of God.

The Father told Jesus He was not only loved but also approved. God was pleased with Him. This is significant, because these words came at the beginning of His ministry, before Jesus had accomplished anything toward His life mission. In fact, after His birth, the Bible records very little about the years of Jesus' life leading up to His baptism. As far as we know, Jesus had not done much, other than growing in His relationship with His Father (see Luke 2:52). Yet the Father declared over Him, "Son, You have My full approval." He was happy, satisfied, and delighted with Jesus—*before* Jesus had done the work God gave Him to do.

This truth contradicts everything our performance-driven culture tells us. The world says, "Achieve so you can be approved." But God says, "You are approved before you achieve." Father God is not focused on what we need to do or fix in our lives. He is focused on how much He delights in us! He knows that the revelation of His love and approval will free us to be the sons and daughters He created us to be.

Every person is created with a yearning for significance. Jesus was no exception. Like us, He needed to know His Father's approval, and it was this approval that empowered Him, as a man, to achieve all He was called to do. The same is true for us. In fact, it is the revelation of God's love and approval in our lives that enables us to achieve freely, not motivated by fear of rejection or punishment but by love. This is what John meant when he wrote: *"There is no fear in love. But perfect love drives out fear, because fear has to do with punishment. The one who fears is not made perfect in love"* (1 John 4:18). God's perfect and unconditional love predates any achievement on our part, which removes fear. We no longer need to work for fear of losing God's love. We are free, because like Jesus, we know who we are—the loved and approved children of God.

THE SPIRIT'S DESCENT

The Father's affirmation of Jesus as the loved and approved Son came alongside empowerment from the Holy Spirit. Luke tells us:

When all the people were being baptized, Jesus was baptized too. And as He was praying, Heaven was opened and the Holy Spirit descended on Him in bodily form like a dove... (Luke 3:21–22).

As He was baptized by John, Jesus prayed. He talked with His Father, and His Father answered not only with a declaration of love but also with the anointing of the Holy Spirit. The Bible does not tell us what Jesus prayed during His baptism, but it's reasonable to guess that, as He looked ahead at His ministry, Jesus was asking His Father for the power to accomplish all He had called Him to do. Jesus was fully human, yet according to the prophecies of Isaiah, as the Messiah He would accomplish some incredible things. Isaiah 61, which Jesus would later quote as an introduction to His ministry (see Luke 4:17–19), says of Him:

The Spirit of the Sovereign Lord is on me, because the Lord has anointed me to proclaim good news to the poor. He has sent me to bind up the brokenhearted, to proclaim freedom for the captives and release from darkness for the prisoners, to proclaim the year of the Lord's favor (Isaiah 61:1–2).

The fulfillment of this prophecy would be no small accomplishment. As the prophet stated, it would be possible only by the anointing of the Holy Spirit. Though Jesus was fully God, He had set aside His deity to become a man, and as a result, He could only accomplish His call by the power of the Spirit. Just like us, He was completely dependent upon the Spirit for all He did during His life on earth. This is why the Father needed to anoint Jesus with the supernatural power of the Spirit in preparation for His earthly ministry. Acts 10:38 clearly explains the origin of Jesus' earthly ministry:

> *You know what has happened throughout the province of Judea, beginning in Galilee after the baptism that John preached—how God anointed Jesus of Nazareth with the Holy Spirit and power, and how he went around doing good and healing all who were under the power of the devil, because God was with him.*

At His baptism, Jesus was anointed and empowered to do the good works of His Father's Kingdom. In this passage, the Greek word *euergeteo*, which is translated as "doing good," can also mean "to bestow benefits."[2] By the power of the Spirit, Jesus bestowed the benefits of the Kingdom on all He met. In His humanity, like us, Jesus needed the anointing power of the Holy Spirit to carry on the work God had assigned to Him.

Though Jesus did have a relationship with God and the Holy Spirit from childhood (see Luke 2:52), as far as we know, it does not seem that He had any special power or abilities until the moment when the Holy Spirit descended on Him like a dove. This was the crucial moment in Jesus' life, the moment when He stepped into His role as Messiah and Savior of the world. Only through the anointing of the Holy Spirit could He fulfill His destiny on earth.

The same is true for us. Not only does the Father have the same love and approval for us as He did for Jesus, but He also empowers us with His Spirit to do the work of the Kingdom. In our humanity, we need the *same anointing* Jesus received. And, as Jesus taught, the empowerment of His followers to do all He did (and more) has been God's plan from the beginning (see John 14:12). Just as Jesus'

---

[2] *Strong's Concordance*, Greek #2109.

work of redemption on the cross was only possible through the Holy Spirit, so too, our work in expanding the Kingdom of God on earth is only possible by God's Spirit. When Jesus returned to Heaven, His job description became ours. He commissioned His followers to take His Kingdom into all the earth, and He sent His Spirit to make it possible (see Acts 1–2).

Our individual parts in fulfilling Christ's commission are only possible when, like Jesus, we experience the two aspects of His baptism—the love and approval of the Father and the empowerment of the Spirit for good works. When we are embraced by our Father's arms, secured in our identity as His beloved children, and when we are overshadowed by His dove, then we will be ready to minister His good news to the world.

THE BLUEPRINT

In this sense, then, Jesus' baptism is a prototype or blueprint that shows what every believer needs. Physical baptism is an important outward sign. It is an image of our spiritual death with Christ and our spiritual rebirth as new creations. However, that is not what is in view in this passage. The baptism Jesus experienced at the Jordan River was a commissioning into ministry; specifically, it was a baptism of identity and power.

This same baptism is a necessary part of every believer's life. If we are baptized only into new life in Christ, but never into a revelation of God's love for us and His power in our lives, we are missing out on a big part of what Jesus died to give us. To be transformed into Christ's image and fulfill our calling on earth, we must experience this baptism of love and power. Through His life on earth, Jesus showed us what it looks like for men, women, and children to be filled with the Spirit and to do the works of the Kingdom in the power of the Holy Spirit, rooted in our identity as children loved by Father God.

It is, of course, one thing to say this and another to experience it. A baptism like Jesus' takes more than a mental assent; it involves an experience that changes us from the inside out. In the New Testament, baptism is used as a symbol for the death of our old selves and the new life we experience in Christ. We die with Him, going under the waters, and we are raised with Him into new life. Paul says it this way:

> Or don't you know that all of us who were baptized into Christ Jesus were baptized into his death? We were therefore buried with him through baptism into death in order that, just as Christ was raised from the dead through the glory of the Father, we too may live a new life. For if we have been united with him in a death like his, we will certainly also be united with him in a resurrection like his (Romans 6:3–5).

This idea of death and resurrection in baptism applies not only to physical baptism and our salvation experience but also to the baptism of the Spirit that we (like Jesus) also need. When Jesus went under the water, He traded His human identity and ability for God's identity and ability. In the same way, through the baptism of the Spirit, we die to our old ideas about ourselves and our old insecurities. As we step into the waters of redemption and ask God to confirm our identity, He will speak to our hearts just as He did to Jesus. By His Spirit, He will help us to release the old identity into the water of God's grace, and we will stand up as beloved and chosen children of God. The old ideas wash off, and we step out into our true identity in our Father.

Likewise, our human ideas of what we can do and the limitations we experience are washed away in the flood of God's power, and we become doers of His works. As we ask Him to fill us with His Spirit and His power, the Spirit will come upon us and empower us with His divine might. Now, His power flows in us, and the old limitations are gone. We are now able to do all that Christ did, and even greater things, because His Spirit lives in us (see John 14:12).

We are new creations, filled with a new belonging and a new power—all because of Christ's work in us. In Ephesians, Paul painted a beautiful picture of this:

> *I pray that out of his glorious riches he may strengthen you with power through his Spirit in your inner being, so that Christ may dwell in your hearts through faith. And I pray that you, being rooted and established in love, may have power, together with all the Lord's holy people, to grasp how wide and long and high and deep is the love of Christ, and to know this love that surpasses knowledge—that you may be filled to the measure of all the fullness of God (Ephesians 3:16–19).*

Paul desired this fullness of the Christian experience for the early believers. God desires the same for us today. Only when we are rooted in our identity and empowered by His Spirit will we live as we were meant to live.

KNOWING WHO WE ARE

Unfortunately, many Christians go through life without experiencing one or both of these realities. Like I did for so many years, they try to measure up to an imagined standard so they can earn God's love through good works. This is a sad and frustrating place to live. Instead, God wants us to know what He thinks about us and to wrap us in His invisible arms of love. The Passion Translation of Psalm 84 gives us a beautiful picture of God's wrap-around arms:

> *God, Your **wrap around presence** is our defense. In Your kindness, look upon the faces of Your anointed ones....For*

the Lord God is brighter than the brilliance of a sunrise!
Wrapping Himself around me *like a shield, He is so generous*
with His gifts of grace and glory! (Psalm 84:9, 11 PT).

This is God's promise to us. Yet, many of us have a very hard time believing it. For a variety of reasons, we find ourselves unlovable, and though we know in our heads that God loves us, we do not really believe it in our hearts. We have a hard time believing He is really as optimistic and positive about us as the Bible says. We think, *Sure, God loves me, because He is God and that's the holy thing to do, but I doubt He really likes or enjoys me.* In this way, we interpret His love as an obligation and miss the reality—that it is the overflow of His heart toward us. Yes, we did nothing to earn it, and it is not based on our performance, but it is based on who we are as His kids. God loves who we are in the truest and most intimate sense. He loves us at our core, and because of that, He is patient with our weaknesses. Truly, He is the best of fathers.

Think of it in terms of human parents. We call God *Father* because our relationship to Him is mirrored in human relationships between parents and their children. Though the image is not perfect, and sometimes it is greatly distorted, good human parents experience a deep and unexplainable love for their children from birth that has nothing to do with anything the child has done. In fact, that child is quite needy, and the parents sacrifice much time and sleep feeding the baby, changing diapers, and soothing the baby to sleep. All parents testify that it is an exhausting job. Yet, the exhaustion is worth it simply because of the parents' love for the child. It is something we cannot quite wrap our minds around, but it is the power of unconditional love. And this is the love God has toward us—and even greater—not just when we are infants but throughout our lives. Through our ups and downs, through the joys and the hurts, He sees walking with us and Fathering us as a joy and a privilege. In fact, He gave the most valuable of gifts in order to free us from sin and restore us to relationship with Him. He would not have done that if we (each one of us) were not worth it to Him.

In light of this, we can trust the revelation of the Father's heart for us in Jeremiah 29:11: *"'For I know the plans I have for you,' declares the Lord, 'plans to prosper you and not to harm you, plans to give you hope and a future.'"* In other words, God promises that He is always available to us. His unseen arms are always present, and we can always experience His embrace. Further, the word translated here as *"plans"* is more accurately translated *"thoughts."*[3] The thoughts God thinks toward us are thoughts of hope and peace and joy. They are thoughts of delight and prosperity. They are the thoughts a good dad thinks toward the children he adores.

The apostle Paul adds to this the reality that *"in Him we live and move and have our being...we are His offspring"* (Acts 17:28). This is the extent of God's love for us. He is so close to us that His presence continually encompasses us. We actually live and exist *in* Him. At all times, we are enveloped in His love; if we were not, we could not continue to exist. It is His heartbeat that both creates and sustains us. Of course, people who have wandered from Him are not aware of His love, but it is always there, always calling to them. And when they return home to His heart, He pours His love into their hearts by the Holy Spirit (see Rom. 5:5).

In the years before I realized God's deep love for me, I lived with the assumption that God was angry, disappointed, and full of regret about me. I thought His thoughts about me primarily focused on my sin and my need for improvement. This, I now know, is a lie. This is thinking that is not aligned with faith in what God says is true. These ungodly beliefs—judgments, opinions, expectations, and beliefs that do not line up with the Word of God—kept me from seeing God's heart accurately. And for many years, they brought

---

[3] *Strong's Concordance*, Hebrew #4284.

destruction into my life and into my relationships with other people and with God Himself.

I am so thankful that God awoke me from my delusion and enabled me to see the truth of who He is and who He says I am. This truth is the anchor of my soul. My Father loves me, forever and always. He loves me. No matter what is happening in my world, He loves me, and He is the safest and kindest person I know. His unseen arms are always available to me. All I need to do is turn toward Him and allow His presence to wrap around me. All I need to do is listen to His declarations of love and truth over me. In Him, like Jesus, I have found who I really am.

OVERFLOWING WITH GOD

As an overflow of my experience of identity in God, I am also now able to overflow with His presence and good works in a way that I never could when I worked so hard in my own strength. Of course, like all believers, I received the Spirit at the moment I accepted Christ's offer of salvation. When we are born again, God brings our spirits to life in our new nature and fills us with His Holy Spirit. At that moment, we receive the fullness of the Godhead (see Col. 2:10). We become one with God, and He dwells in us. About this, Paul says: *"Whoever is united with the Lord is one with him in spirit"* (1 Cor. 6:17). And John also testifies: *"The one who keeps God's commands lives in him, and he in them. And this is how we know that he lives in us: We know it by the Spirit he gave us"* (1 John 3:24).

This is the reality for every believer. Yet many of us have not learned how to live in that reality. Whether it's because of a lack of biblical teaching, unresolved inner wounds, or a personal desire to maintain control of our lives, many of us chose to live in bondage even though Christ has given us freedom. For me, it was all of the above. The result is only more pain and oppression. The result is somewhat like receiving a multi-million dollar inheritance and yet living in poverty on the streets. This is how I lived for eleven miserable years. I was a Christian, and if had I died, I believe I would have gone to Heaven. I had received eternal life, yet I was not experiencing eternal life in this life, as Jesus intended. I had little joy, no real peace, and a lot of self-reliance.

I had not grown up in the church, and when I accepted Christ, the denomination I belonged to did not teach about the Holy Spirit. Add to that the fact that I was deeply wounded, full of insecurity, and extremely driven. My paradigm for what it meant to be a Christian was all wrong, mostly because no one had ever shown me the truth about the freedom Christ gives us through His Spirit. I thought once one was saved one must keep working really hard, but in the name of Jesus. I did not know He had given me His Spirit and the grace (divine empowerment) I needed to work for Him from a place of peace and joy.

Not until God began speaking to me about returning to His love (as I shared in the Introduction) did this false paradigm begin to change. Following His lead, I discovered the pure, satisfying, abundant, life-giving love of my heavenly Daddy. This was the love I had searched for all my life. As I received the revelation of God's love for me and my identity in Him, I began to desire the baptism of the Holy Spirit. I did not even know what that looked like, but I knew I wanted to experience the fullness of relationship with God. I wanted to live in all that Christ had died to give me. I read about the lives of the early believers in the Book of Acts, and I wanted to walk in that kind of divine strength and power. I wanted to be an ordinary person filled with the boldness and courage of Christ. I wanted to see the signs and wonders, the salvations and miracles, the supernatural provision, the healthy and loving relationships. Reading the Book of Acts, I saw a picture of the abundant life in Christ, and I realized I was not living in that reality.

This, of course, was not because I had an inferior salvation to that of the early believers. It was simply because I had not experienced the baptism of the Spirit and stepped into the fullness of all Christ had provided for me. When I realized that, I found myself plunging into the baptismal waters for a fuller experience of the Father's love and empowerment in my life. Following in the footsteps of Christ, I heard my Father's affirmation of me as His beloved daughter, and I received the empowerment of His Spirit to do the works of the Kingdom. At last, I was ready and able to be commissioned into my destiny as one who represents my Father on earth.

At last I had stepped into the reality the apostle Paul describes as the norm for every believer:

Do not get drunk on wine, which leads to debauchery. Instead, be filled with the Spirit, speaking to one another with psalms, hymns, and songs from the Spirit. Sing and make music from your heart to the Lord, always giving thanks to God the Father for everything, in the name of our Lord Jesus Christ (Ephesians 5:18–20).

Living life in the Spirit is not a one-time event but a daily reality. It is the new normal that results from the baptism of the Spirit. Instead of being filled and influenced by earthly realities, we get to be filled and overflowing with the very Spirit of God. Though I once was filled with lies that brought me pain and despair, I am now filled with the Spirit of life. This is the real source of joy and peace—being filled to overflowing with the love of God. Paul prayed, *"May the God of hope fill you with all joy and peace as you trust in Him, so that you may overflow with hope by the power of the Holy Spirit"* (Rom. 15:13). This reality is available to each one of us. It is part of our inheritance, already purchased for us and delivered to us through the death and resurrection of Jesus. This is our Father's will and desire for each one of us—overflowing love, hope, joy, peace, trust. This is good news! He offers to all believers the same baptism of identity and power that Jesus received. It is available, and it is essential. We are not powerless orphan-slaves. We are sons and daughters of God, with all the authority of His name.

Truth Declarations

I AM ALWAYS LOVED BY MY FATHER!

Father loves me with an everlasting love. I have always been loved by Him (see Jer. 31:3).

Father loves me so much that He gave His only Son to die for me so I might experience His love (see John 3:16).

Father loves me just as much as He loves Jesus (see John 17:23).

Father loves me so much He wants to express His love and affection to me (see John 16:27).

Nothing can separate me from God's love for me (see Rom. 8:39).

Even when I have sinned, the Father forgives me, loves me, and asks me to sit beside Him with Jesus. I am seated in the Heavenly realms now (see Eph. 2:4–6).

Father desires me to overflow in His love (see Eph. 3:19).

Father's countless thoughts towards me are always good (see Ps. 139:17).

I AM FILLED WITH THE SPIRIT OF GOD, AND HE EMPOWERS ME!

The Holy Spirit is a like a flowing, living, surging river within me. I am invited to continually drink from Him (see John 7:39).

I am empowered to drive out all fear with the perfect love of God (see 1 John 4:18).

I have the same anointing of the Spirit that Jesus carried. His job description has become mine in our Father's family business (see John 14:12).

I have been given authority to drive out demons and heal the sick (see Matt. 10:1).

I am filled with the Spirit of life. He is the real source of joy, peace, and hope. He is my constant companion. I choose to be filled to overflowing all throughout my day (see Eph. 5:18–20; Rom. 15:13).

Jesus is counting on me to synchronize earth with the Kingdom of Heaven—healing the sick, raising the dead, cleansing the lepers, and casting out demons (see Matt. 10:7–8).

Like Jesus, I am anointed with the same Holy Spirit and power to go around doing good, bestowing the benefits of the Kingdom, and healing all those under the power of the devil, for God is with me (see Acts 10:38).

The Holy Spirit who raised Jesus from the dead is living in me, since my salvation. He will give life to my mortal body because He dwells within me (see Rom. 8:11).

GETTING PERSONAL

1. Slowly read Matthew 3:13–17. Pray something like this: *"Father, thank You for the Spirit of wisdom and revelation to know and experience You. Please open the eyes of my heart to encounter Your love and be filled with Your power."*

Imagine yourself in this biblical scene with Jesus. Invite the Holy Spirit to descend upon you and to rest on you like He did Jesus. With your heart fixed on Him, listen carefully to the Father as He speaks His words of love and affirmation over you. Envision the Holy Spirit coming to rest on you as a dove and empowering you with His might. Record what you sense God is saying and showing you.

_____

_____

_____

_____

2. Before reading this book, what did you assume God was thinking about you? Has that changed? How? Write down any negative assumptions you had about God's thoughts toward you. Then write down the truth that counters that lie.

_____

_____

_____

_____

_____

_____

_____

3. What have you come to appreciate most about the Father's unseen arms reaching toward you?

_____

_____

_____

4. Using the Truth Declarations from this chapter, meditate on what Father God really thinks about you. Regularly declare these truths from the Bible over yourself to renew your mind to God's way of thinking (see Rom. 12:2). Look up these truths in your Bible and dialogue with the Lord by asking, *"Father, what do You want to say to me about this truth?"* Write what He says here:

_____

_____

_____

_____

CHAPTER 3

Inheritance Received

When a Jewish teacher of the law asked Jesus which of the Old Testament commandments was the *most* important, Jesus responded with what is commonly called the Great Commandment:

Love the Lord your God with all your heart and with all your soul and with all your mind and with all your strength. The second is this: Love your neighbor as yourself. There is no commandment greater than these (Mark 12:30–31).

Instead of telling this man to perform a certain religious duty, Jesus pointed him toward love. First of all, love God. Second, love others. Jesus was declaring to a culture obsessed with rules that a heart of love matters to God more than anything a person might do. This was the foundation of the gospel embedded in the old covenant, which Jesus came to unveil in the new covenant. Thus, toward the end of His ministry, Jesus gave His disciples a new command about love. He told them that the standard for love was no longer how much they loved themselves (as it says in Mark 12) but how much He loves them. According to the old covenant, they were only obligated to love others as much as they loved themselves. Now, as they faced the beginning of the new covenant, Jesus told them they could actually love others as much as He loves them.[4]

Three times during Jesus' teaching in John 13–17, directly before His arrest and death, Jesus explained this new standard for love to His disciples. First, He said:

A new command I give you: Love one another. As I have loved you, so you must love one another. By this everyone will know that you are my disciples, if you love one another (John 13:34–35).

Then, again, He repeated this new command, using it to foreshadow the ultimate act of love that He was about to commit on the cross: *"My command is this: Love each other as I have loved you. Greater love has no one than this: to lay down one's life for one's friends"* (John 15:12–13). Then, a third time, Jesus repeated the command to love, this time identifying it as the fruit His disciples are called to bear:

You did not choose me, but I chose you and appointed you so that you might go and bear fruit—fruit that will last—and so that whatever you ask in my name the Father will give you. This is my command: Love each other (John 15:16–17).

This is a profound revelation. And it is the foundation of the new covenant message, the new covenant law of love. We were made to be loved by God, and from that experience of His love to love others in the same way.

---

[4] I first heard this idea from Jonathan Welton, *Understanding the Whole Bible* (Rochester, NY: Welton Academy, 2014), pg. 329.

When I discovered the Father's love for me, my life changed drastically. As I began to mature in this love relationship with my Father, His love became the *catalyst* within me, enabling me to *love Him back* and to love others with His love. The more I experience the Father's love, the more I learn about how to receive and give healthy love. This is what it means to be transformed into His image (see Rom. 12:2; 2 Cor. 3:18). This is the essence of our faith, the foundation for everything else we do.

MADE FOR LOVE

As we have discussed in the first two chapters of this book, God's lavish love knows no bounds, is without limit, is unconditional, and will never fail us. He is always with us, reaching out to embrace us, whether we are behaving or not. His love is the most amazing gift—one He created us to receive. Before we did anything to please Him, He loved us. It is as John says: *"We love because he first loved us"* (1 John 4:19). Love was His idea, and He reached out to us first. Only in Christianity do we find a God who reaches out and pursues His creation. Every other religion teaches that people are responsible to reach out to God. The truth is, God continually reaches toward us, wooing our hearts with His kindness. All we need to do is to acknowledge, accept, and experience the reality of the gift He has given us through Jesus Christ.

In my own life, I am beginning to experience how multifaceted and unending my Father's love is for me. He is always with me, and He has given me the fullness of new covenant life—yet I am still learning to live in His presence and manifest His Kingdom. The more time I spend in His presence, the more I become aware of all He has given me. The more I experience His love, the more I long to know Him in fullness. The more I experience His love, the more He renews my mind to who I really am in Him, and the more He enables me to live as the amazing person He created me to be. Life has become, for me, a progressive revelation of my identity as a co-heir with Christ (see Rom. 8:17). The enemy is eternally defeated, and he no longer has the power to control me (see Col. 2:15). Instead, I *"reign in life through the one man, Jesus Christ"* (Rom. 5:17).

What a contrast this has been to the first years of my Christian life. Not until my late thirties did I realized how hard my heart had become. I grew up with wonderful parents who loved each other and loved my brother and me. Yet, because of a series of traumatic events in my early life, I learned as a young child to protect myself at all costs. I built walls all around me. When people would try to get close to me, I rebuffed them. I did not want anyone to have access to my heart. Instead, I believed:

- I can't trust people; they only want something from me.

- Loving others causes me great pain.

- I can keep people at a distance to protect myself from being hurt.

- I must reject others before they reject me.

- If things get difficult, I should cut my losses and run.

Of course, while this does apply to some people, it does not apply to most. Yet, because of the fear and pain in my life, I found it safer to apply it to all people in hopes of avoiding the bad ones. For nearly four decades, I lived with this framework of deep skepticism and mistrust for others. I was clueless about how to even receive love, let alone give it. What I thought was my demonstration of love was actually demanding, conditional, and inconsistent. It was not love at all, but I was unwilling to see that, because I had used the pain in my heart to justify my choices and viewpoint.

Not surprisingly, the first few years of my marriage were horrible. Both Richard and I came into the marriage with a lot of emotional baggage, and after we were married, we created collective baggage. In my deepest of hearts, I wanted be to loved, yet I was terrified of being hurt and rejected, so I refused to let any love get through. I did not have room for love in my heart, because it was filled with fear and pain. Driven by self-destruction, I tried on numerous occasions to persuade Richard to get a divorce. At the same time, I knew something was wrong, and I desperately wanted to change. I just didn't know how. Then, I met Jesus!

Though Jesus had become my Savior, the walls barricading my heart remained. Some of them softened, but many of them were my closest allies. It's hard, even for Jesus, to have a relationship with someone who has walls like I did. I only had so much capacity for His love. Because I didn't believe He really loved me unless I worked hard and somehow measured up to His standards, I held Him at arm's length. But Jesus was patient. As I described in Chapter 1, eventually Jesus broke through those walls, and for the first time, I was able to experience the love God had always had for me. When I came to the end of my own strength, I discovered that my Father's arms had been surrounding me all along. I just did not know He was there. I did not know what His love was like or how to allow myself to receive it.

I had no idea that God is, as Paul puts it, *"the Father of compassion and the God of all comfort"* (2 Cor. 1:3) and could heal my broken places. When I discovered His healing love, I realized that in every circumstance of my life, the compassionate and comforting Father desires to come alongside me and listen, encourage, console, reassure, calm, strengthen, and counsel me. He wants to share Himself with me, no matter what's going on in my life. In fact, this is one of the main things the Father does for us. It's His specialty. The Old Testament prophet Zephaniah described this aspect of the Father like this:

The LORD your God is with you, the Mighty Warrior who saves. He will take great delight in you; in his love he will no longer rebuke you, but will rejoice over you with singing (Zephaniah 3:17).

This is exactly what He did for me. He gathered me up like a broken little child and held me closely, breaking through to the core of my being with His love, compassion, and mercy. He gladly filled me with the power of His love and the Spirit. Over the course of several intense years, He mended the broken places in my heart, quieted me with His love, enabled me to hear His songs of deliverance, and celebrated with me every step of the way. He also brought people into my life who had also received His compassion, comfort, and healing, and they walked alongside me. They were a safe place, and they patiently pointed me to God for help in working through the baggage.

Now, looking back at that season, I can say I have truly come to know the Father and His comfort, and I have experienced the healing only He can bring. He did not demand instant change or look down on me for my struggles. Instead, He gently and tenderly dismantled the protective walls I had built and breathed new life into the wounded and hard parts of my heart. Though I am not finished learning about His love (I never will be), I am now whole and at peace in Him. The more I grow in His love, the more I learn about the second part of the new covenant law of love—loving others as He loves me.

MADE TO LOVE

God made us for love, but as we receive His love, we become vessels of His love, and we begin to pour that love out on the world around us. That is the natural result of being loved by God. Paul makes this progression clear when He refers to *"the Father of compassion and the God of all comfort"*:

Praise be to the God and Father of our Lord Jesus Christ, the Father of compassion and the God of all comfort, who comforts us in all our troubles, so that we can comfort those in any trouble with the comfort we ourselves receive from God (2 Corinthians 1:3–4).

These two ideas are inseparable. First, we receive the love of the Father, and as a result, we love others with that same love. In fact, Paul says we receive love *so that* we can love. Our own love relationship with God, as important as it is, is not the end goal. Instead, as God fills us with His love, He invites us to step outside of ourselves and, like Him, to begin pouring ourselves out for others. We don't do this on our own strength or with our own love, but strengthened and empowered with His love. It is like the loaves of bread and fish that Jesus used to feed the crowds. The small lunch, enough for one person, multiplied into sustenance for thousands, with leftovers. In the same way, the love poured into a single human heart is multiplied over and over; it is handed out here and there to bring life to many.

This is the heart of our Father. He comforts, encourages, and strengthens us *so that* we can take that same comfort and freely give it away to others. As we become whole in His love, He commissions us to take His love to the world. Sharing His love with the world is possible only when we first receive His love. We cannot give away what we do not have.

Unfortunately, many Christians serve, perform, and strive from a place of emptiness. Immediately before Christ ascended into Heaven, He commissioned His followers to spread the Kingdom throughout the world:

All authority in heaven and on earth has been given to me. Therefore go and make disciples of all nations, baptizing them in the name of the Father and of the Son and of the Holy Spirit, and teaching them to obey everything I have commanded you. And surely I am with you always, to the very end of the age (Matthew 28:18–20).

Many Christians are rightly passionate about fulfilling this incredible mandate from Jesus. We should be driven to share the gospel with those who need to hear it. We should be compelled to love as Christ loves. The problem is when we make the Great Commission more important than our personal intimacy with God. Many believers have these two foundations of life with God out of order, and because of this, they are trying to fulfill the Great Commission on their own strength, without first being filled to overflowing with God's love. The truth is, if we have not yet experienced the life-changing love of God and received healing in our hearts, from the inside out, we are incapable of truly loving others. To give real love, we first must be filled with that love from our Father.

When I first became a Christian, because of my inner pain, I was terrified of receiving ministry or love from others, let alone from God. Even the idea of it made me feel terribly vulnerable; so instead, I busied myself serving. After all, if I was the one serving, I didn't need to worry about someone trying to minister to me. I used the busyness of ministry—helping others, building programs, making sandwiches Jesus didn't order—to keep a lid on my bottled-up pain. Like me, people who live this way become exhausted, weary, and bored. We can only travel so far on empty.

Over the years since my personal encounter with God's love, I have had the privilege of coming alongside many individuals, couples, and ministry leaders from all over the country. Like me, they had been serving fervently for years without realizing they were missing a key piece of their inheritance as a child of God. They didn't know about the Father's heart, His love, and His power. They didn't know they could have a relationship with all three members of the Godhead. Some of them were tight with Jesus, but they didn't know the Father. Some knew the Father but believed He was distant. For some, the Holy Spirit wasn't even on their radar. They had no idea they could be *"filled to the measure of all the fullness of God"* (Eph. 3:19). But once they encountered Father God and tasted His love, everything changed. The weariness and need to perform left, and they were finally free and able to receive God's love and also to serve people with the overflow of that love.

A few years ago, a young woman name Michelle made an appointment with me to talk about the direction of her life and her desire to serve Jesus wholeheartedly. I was drawn to her the moment we met. She was really smart, well versed in the Bible, and contagiously enthusiastic about making a difference for the Lord. She was feisty and inspiring! As we talked about her life and dreams, she eventually shared with me the frustration she felt about her spiritual life. She had been serving in a ministry that was focused on the Great Commission but, unfortunately, had not taught her very much about intimacy with God.

She had begun to feel dissatisfied with her Christian life because it did not look at all like the apostle Paul's. Paul seemed to be continually led by the Spirit. She wondered, *How did he know it was the Spirit? Was it an audible voice? Did he feel a push? Or was he just a super Christian who was gifted with the ability to always hear God's voice?* Unwilling to believe Paul had a special lifestyle that was unavailable to the rest of us, she began to pray, "Lord teach me how to be led by the Spirit." Though she wasn't sure exactly what she was asking for, she knew she wanted what Paul had.

As Michelle and I talked, we both began to sense that God was up to something big in this meeting. It wasn't long until she was in tears. As the peace of God permeated the room, I asked her,

"Michelle, how important do you think it is to know how to hear the voice of the Lord?"

She paused. Later, she told me that this question had caught her off guard. After all, she prayed every day and had read through the Bible. She had memorized hundreds of Bible verses and regularly told people about Jesus. *I'm not spiritually stupid,* she thought. *Of course I think it's important.* But then she realized the truth. Looking at me with something akin to amazement, she said, "Apparently not that important, or you wouldn't be asking me the question."

What Michelle had realized in that moment was that her theology of God was based on working to earn His love. The very thing she lacked and longed for was an intimate relationship with Him in which she was led by His revelatory voice and heard His perspective and answers to the questions on her heart. For so long, she had taken pride in over-analyzing and creating answers to life questions on her own. While she talked to God and asked Him questions, she did not know how to listen to the still small voice of God, and she did not really expect Him to answer. She was so busy finding her own solutions that she didn't know how to be still and connect with His heart.

This realization was the beginning of a transformation. Instead of being self-led, Michelle began to be Spirit-led. Instead of living by the evidence, she began living by faith, and she learned to respond to crisis with peace instead of fear. She no longer sought to simply understand God with her mind but to love Him with her heart. All this happened because of an encounter with love. At the bottom of Michelle's struggle was a void in her heart. Like me, she needed to meet her heavenly Father and experience His lavish love. When she finally did, she discovered how easy it is to serve and love people from a place of overflow.

OVERFLOWING WITH LOVE

To be effective followers of Jesus, we must live from this place of overflow. All we do and who we are must result from the love we receive from our Father. In the Book of Acts, we find a great example of what this looks like. In the early days of the church, not long after the outpouring at Pentecost, Peter and John encountered a crippled man on the way to the temple in Jerusalem. This man, who had been crippled from birth, sat and begged outside one of the temple gates. Seeing Peter and John, he called out to them, asking for money. Peter, seeing this man's need for something greater than money, responded from the overflow of God's love in his life. He said, *"Silver or gold I do not have, but what I do have I give you. In the name of Jesus Christ of Nazareth, walk"* (Acts 3:6). Grabbing him by the hand, Peter helped the man to his feet, and instantly he was healed. When the man's celebrations of his healing drew the attention of the crowds, Peter said to them, *"Why do you stare at us as if by our own power or godliness we had made this man walk?"* (Acts 3:12). Then, he explained the good news of the new covenant to them, and thousands of people turned to the Lord.

Peter knew his ability to help the crippled man and share the gospel did not come from his own strength or goodness. Instead, it came from the love of God flowing into his heart and overflowing out of him to the world in need. Because Peter prioritized his relationship with God above anything else, he lived from a place of fullness, and he knew how to release what God had put within him. In other words, he knew how to be a conduit of the Father's love within. Because he knew who he was as a loved son and he had the power of the Spirit living in Him, he was able to release God's supernatural solution for this man's need. As he and other believers regularly met together and encountered God together, they were filled again and again with the Spirit (see Acts 2:4; 4:31). It is not surprising, then, that later in Acts we see people being healed simply as Peter walked by them (see Acts 5:15–16). He was so filled up with the love and power of God that powerful demonstrations of God's love followed in his wake.

This should be the norm for every believer. We were made for love, and we were made to love. It's that simple. And when we allow ourselves to experience God's love for us, loving others becomes simple. It becomes the overflow of our relationship with our Father. It becomes the natural expression of who we are as His beloved kids.

Truth Declarations

I HAVE GREAT PURPOSE IN MY FATHER!

I carry the Kingdom of God within me everywhere I go (see Luke 17:21).

I can hear my Father's voice and follow His lead (see John 10:27).

Because of my faith in Jesus, the Holy Spirit will empower me to do greater works than Jesus (see John 14:12).

Father God does not give me fear. He doesn't give what He doesn't have. I am filled with power, love, and a sound mind (see 2 Tim. 1:7).

The Holy Spirit will reveal to me the mind and heart of my Father as I look to Him (see 1 Cor. 2:10).

I live from the overflow of God's love for me. I was created to be deeply loved by God. I choose to be a good receiver of His love and to give it away freely. Only He can show me what healthy love really looks like (see John 15:16–17).

Jesus faithfully points me to my inheritance of love (see Mark 12:30–31).

In the new covenant, Jesus has reconciled me with my Father based on a relationship of love, not religious duty and rules (see Rom. 7:6).

The standard of love is based on how much He loves. God is love. I can love others as much as He loves them (see John 13:34–35; 15:12).

My Father of compassion and comfort desires to share Himself fully with me to heal the broken places in my heart with His healing love (see 2 Cor. 1:3).

I am the delight of my Father. He rejoices over me with singing (see Zeph. 3:17).

Out of the intimacy and fullness of God's love for me, I can truly love others (see Eph. 3:19).

I live in the overflow of God's love in my life. He gives me divine wisdom and solutions to give away to others in need (see Acts 3:6).

GETTING PERSONAL

1. If you desire a greater experience of the Father's love for you, place your hand on your heart, quiet your mind and emotions, and pray this prayer with faith and expectation:

> "Father God—Papa—I want to know You and experience Your lavish love for me. I know You have adopted me as Your beloved child and given me access to Your heart. I'm not sure what that looks like, but I say yes to Your love. I'm sorry for putting up walls and trying to protect myself, not realizing how much You love me. I'm sorry for serving You and others from a place of brokenness. Father of comfort, please teach me about Your true love, and then teach me how to release that love to others."

2. Slowly read and meditate on 1 John 3:1 and 4:19. In what ways has the Father *lavished* His love upon you?

_____

_____

_____

_____

3. In what ways can you make encountering God's love a greater priority in your life? Are there areas where you have tried to serve Him or others from a place of lack instead of fullness?

_____

_____

_____

_____

4. Have you met the Father of all Comfort and allowed Him to heal you from the inside out? Ask Him, *"Father, what do You want to say to me regarding the broken places in my heart?"*

_____

_____

_____

_____

5. You cannot give what you don't have. Ask God, *"Father, what are You revealing to me through Peter's example?"*

_____

_____

_____

_____

6. When you pray, which member of the Trinity do you relate to most? What is your relationship with the other two members of the Godhead? Take a moment and ask *"Lord, what do You want to say to me right now about my relationship with You?"*

_____

_____

_____

_____

CHAPTER 4

Overcomer

In 2011, my husband, Richard, accepted a job two states away from where we lived. Initially, the job was supposed to last just two months, but it turned into a full year of living apart, with only weekends together. This was very hard on us, because we weren't used to being apart. On the weekends, we would try to live as much life as we could before he headed back. During this time, he also had two major accidents while cycling. First, he was mugged. And later, a homeless man walked out in front of him, and in the resulting crash, Richard suffered a collapsed lung and broken ribs. Healing and recovering, both physically and emotionally, took some time.

In the end, Richard decided to end his employment with this company. The cost of being apart simply was not worth it. For the following year, Richard was unemployed. We shifted from one extreme to the other. First, he was gone nearly all the time, and then he was home without a job. Neither situation was easy for us, but in the midst of that difficult season, God taught me something valuable about abiding in my Father's love. When we face difficult times, we always have a choice. Will we run to our Father's arms, which are always there, for comfort and strength? Or will we rely on our own understanding?

About three and a half months into Richard's out-of-state job, I realized I had been internalizing my resentment about being alone. On the weekends, we focused on being together, but during the week I focused on keeping busy with ministry and activity. Inside, I felt depressed and tired. These feelings were an old default that I had become used to in former seasons of my life. I didn't like that I was returning to that place, but it was familiar and easy. Then, one morning while I was spending time with Jesus, I heard Him whisper to my heart, inviting me to pour out what I had been holding back. As I described to Him my feelings of weariness and loneliness, I sensed Him saying:

"Vikki, I know you are trying to be strong, but you don't have to do this by yourself. I want to give you a breakthrough in the area of discouragement. The enemy wants to rob you and bring loss into your life. He has tried this many times since your childhood, and he knows it has worked. The truth is that you are an overcomer because I live on the inside of you. Step into this reality, choose to draw a line in the sand, and say *no* to discouragement for good. I want you to press into the abundant life that only I can give. Abundant life is My part. Your part is to receive, embrace, enjoy, give it back to me, receive more, give it away, and receive more by stewarding expectancy and hope."

This was exactly what I needed to hear. According to John, *"Everyone born of God overcomes the world. This is the victory that has overcome the world, even our faith"* (1 John 5:4). When we are born again, we receive the ability to overcome in all circumstances in life. We are no longer under the power of the enemy or the oppression that fills the world apart from Christ. This is our reality as new creations. However, to live in this reality as overcomers, we need to practice turning to Christ in the midst of difficulty. We need to rewire our hearts and minds to the truth of God's Word instead of believing the lies of our circumstances. In effect, we are creating a new default pattern. This is the process the apostle Paul calls "renewing our minds" (see Rom. 12:2).

In the situation with Richard's job, I had a choice. I could steward discouragement, or I could steward life through expectancy and hope. I chose the latter and decided from that day onward to be an overcomer. In the years since then, I have learned more and more to steward hope in my life and to ignore hopelessness and discouragement. And I have seen the fruit of this choice over and over. The year when Richard was unemployed was very difficult for us financially. Yet we chose to trust God's promises and to run to Him with our struggles. And God transformed our difficulty into an upgrade. Not only did He provide for us in a variety of ways, but He enabled Richard to follow his dream and start his own company. Also, He helped us to see that season as an opportunity to strengthen our marriage and reconnect with each other in a way that would not have been possible if Richard had been working full time.

From this we learned, like never before, that when we return to our Father's unseen arms, we receive an infusion of His hope for our lives. He is never discouraged or hopeless. No situation is beyond His redemption. The question is, will we agree with His perspective, or will we empower a false and negative perspective on our lives? If we agree with the lies of the enemy, we hinder our own breakthrough and keep ourselves from living in the fullness of our inheritance in God.

Recently, God spoke to me about the power of seeing my life from His perspective. Occasionally, I will look back at old prayer journals to remind myself of the answered prayers and direction I received from God in those seasons. As I was doing so, the Holy Spirit showed me that for many years my journals were filled with a continual pleading for the same needs—my marriage, my relationships, my parenting, my finances, and so forth. For years, I had spent much of my prayer life begging God to meet the same needs without realizing that He has already provided the solutions for every dilemma I face. Our Father knows our needs, and He meets them (see Matt. 6:7–8, 31–33). We don't have to beg Him. Instead, we can trust in His goodness and focus on seeing our lives from His perspective. When we do, we will begin to use our authority to access the storehouses in Heaven for the answers to our prayers— and also for needs that transcend our own personal lives. After all, our purpose in life is bringing the atmosphere of the Kingdom from Heaven to earth. So often we get stuck in a bubble of our own need that keeps us from impacting the world. The answer to this is simple: know who we are and live from Heaven's perspective.

When we do this, we will overcome. God wants to increase our revelation of our identity so that we can overcome in any situation we face. We possess the fullness of victory in Him. We have already overcome, because we share in Jesus' victory over sin and death. But we always have a choice about whether we will live in the victory He has already given us. God does not force us to overcome. He does not force us to say no to discouragement and hopelessness. He has provided all we need to rise above those lies, and they are not part of our new nature in Him. Yet, we still have a choice. And sadly, many of us chose to wallow in hopelessness instead of trusting by faith in the never-failing hope that is in Christ.

KINGDOM OPPORTUNISTS

God wants us to grow from glory to glory in our relationship with Him and our revelation of who we are as His kids. Every situation in our lives, whether good or bad, is an opportunity to grow in these ways. When life is wonderful and happy, we get to learn to cultivate our relationship with Him because of love, not because we need something from Him. In the difficult times, we get to learn how to turn to Him for comfort and how to believe His truth even when we don't see it manifested. Life is all about our perception. Every blessing and every challenge we face brings an opportunity to increase in the Father's love. When we recognize this, we can live as Kingdom opportunists who always take advantage of an opportunity for growth.

Paul tells us that *"in all things God works for the good of those who love him"* (Rom. 8:28). And Jesus promises that, though we often experience trouble and difficulty in this world, He has overcome it all (see John 16:33). That means, when life is hard, we can turn the challenges we face into opportunities to experience a greater revelation of the Father's love and comfort in our lives. In our weakness, He shows off His strength. Like Jesus did when He was in the Garden of Gethsemane, in our hard times, we must learn to turn to our Father. While God is not the author of hard times or suffering in our lives, He is good enough to bring good out of any situation (see John 10:10; Rom. 8:28). Even when other people attack us and seek to harm us, God can redeem what they meant for evil. However, often this redemption hinges on our choice to turn to Him and trust in His goodness in our lives.

If, instead, we try to fix the problem in our own strength or respond with fear, anger, hopelessness, or other toxic emotions, we are effectively telling God we want to handle it on our own. And He'll let us try it that way. He never forces us to run to Him. But when we chose anything other than running to His unseen arms and trusting in His goodness and grace, we miss out on the redemption He wants to bring into every difficult situation we face. When we do this, we actually sabotage our own growth process and miss out on our opportunity to practice overcoming.

This is why it is so important, when life gets hard, to see ourselves at a crossroads and to deliberately choose to position ourselves in the awareness of God's love for us and His Spirit within us. When we, as the Message Bible puts it, have *"nothing between us and God, our faces shining with the brightness of His face,"* then *"we are transfigured much like the Messiah, our lives gradually becoming brighter and more beautiful as God enters our lives and we become like Him"* (2 Cor. 3:18 MSG). This is what it means to have the fullness of God dwelling within us and to be continually renewing our minds to His reality. From that place, we can see that God has a solution for every difficulty, and He has already given us all we need to overcome.

THE OVERCOMER'S KEYS

Knowing who we are as beloved children of God, who have already received the fullness of the Kingdom here on earth, we must learn how to consistently live in that victory. Following are several keys that will help us live like the overcomers God has made us to be.

1. Intimacy with Papa

The first step is simply cultivating our love relationship with our Father. His love for us is limitless, but we grow in our experience of it. The more we experience, the more our faith grows to believe wholeheartedly the truth of the Bible. We find an example of this in Jesus' life in Matthew 16–17. At the end of His ministry loomed the cross, and after a certain point, Jesus began to focus on explaining the coming difficulty to His disciples (see Matt. 16:21). Obviously, Jesus' situation was unique, in that He embraced suffering as the will of the Father in order to bring salvation to humanity. However, that was Jesus' mission alone. Only He is the Savior and the Slain Lamb. We have a different mission on earth, to spread the good news of the Kingdom, and God does not bring suffering into our lives to accomplish that (or for any other purpose). Yes, sometimes we face suffering, but it is not at the Father's hand (see John 10:10). His will for us is always peace and prosperity in all areas of life.

Yet when we do face suffering, we can look to Jesus' example. As His mind was filled with the coming cross, Jesus sought out His Father, and the Father once again affirmed Him with words of love. In the presence of Peter, James, and John, Jesus was transfigured into His heavenly body, momentarily, and the Father audibly said: *"This is my Son, whom I love; with him I am well pleased. Listen to him"* (Matt. 17:5). As a human, Jesus must have been acutely aware of the physical and emotional pain that lay before Him. He would be falsely accused, face an unjust trial, and then be cruelly beaten and crucified. Ultimately, He would rise from the dead, but between that victory and Jesus' present lay a road full of suffering. This was no easy thing for Him to face, as is so clear in His prayer in the Garden of Gethsemane (see Matt. 26:36–46).

In those moments, Jesus faced a greater personal need than ever before. His response to that need is an example to us. He chose to climb the mountain for a special encounter with His Father. There, enveloped by the Father and the Spirit, Jesus received a fresh revelation of love and a fresh resolve to walk forward in the power of the Spirit. By drawing closer to the Father and receiving His loving affirmation, Jesus received the strength He needed to continue forward in faith, trusting in the goodness of His Father.

This was how Jesus lived His life—not just when the cross loomed large but at all times. We see this in His persistent choice to get alone with His Father and cultivate their love relationship (see Matt. 14:23; Mark 1:35; 6:46; Luke 5:16; 6:12; John 6:15). Though Jesus had existed eternally with the Father and had a perfect love relationship with Him, He still chose to spend time with Him. That's what people do when they love. When Jesus found Himself in situations where He needed renewal, strength, direction, or fellowship, He could immediately and simply experience His Father's embrace. He had cultivated a pattern of dwelling in the Father's love. It was His daily reality, and it can be ours, too. When we chose to consciously live in the awareness of God's love and our identity in Him, we position ourselves for a greater revelation of His love and a more consistent ability to overcome.

As we develop a lifestyle of loving and being loved in our relationship with God, we are building a foundation to build our lives upon. It is a default pattern that enables us to make good choices in the midst of crisis. Having our life action plan in place before crisis hits enables us to make the best choice. When turning to God is normal and easy for us, He will be the first one we run to when life gets hard. When we are used to being saturated with His goodness, love, and glory, we will know how to live there in the midst of chaos and confusion. This is true transformation. Our minds are renewed in God's presence and by believing His Word. As a result, the mental pathways in our brains are rearranged, and what used to be our default survival tactics or coping mechanisms changes. Now, the unseen arms of our Father become our new default.

2. Childlike Trust

The second key to living as an overcomer in adversity is maintaining childlike trust in God, even when we do not understand what is happening around us. Again, Jesus is the model for this. In Matthew 26, in the Garden of Gethsemane, as Jesus wrestled with the need for His suffering, He simply chose to trust the goodness of His Father. He prayed, *"My Father, if it is not possible for this cup to be taken away unless I drink it, may your will be done"* (Matt. 26:42). Jesus had to trust the good intentions of His Father, and so do we.

Too often, when we face difficulties, our first response is to look for someone to blame. Often, we ask God *why*, which can turn into offense at Him for the struggles we face. This is not fair; it is not a good way to cultivate trust in our relationship with Him. The truth is, though we do not always know why things happen, we can trust that God is not causing evil in our lives because that's what the Bible tells us. When bad things happen, it's not His fault. That idea is rooted in a victim mindset that looks outward for blame instead of looking inward for a solution.

The reality is that God has given us the power to overcome. When the enemy attacks us, we are empowered with the Spirit of God to stand up and say *no* to destruction in our lives. This is our privilege and responsibility as children of God. Yet we still live in an imperfect world, and life does not always turn out how we expect. Even when we pray with great faith, sometimes we do not see the results we wanted. This does not mean God did not want blessing or healing or breakthrough in that area. The bottom line is this: When we don't understand why something does or does not happen, we must cling to the truth of God's goodness as revealed in the Bible. This is what Jesus did in the Garden. He understood the divine plan of God, yet it seems in His humanity He still longed for a different way.

Jesus also had to trust in the promise of the Father. As a human, He faced death with only the promise that His Father would raise Him back to life. Jesus did not raise Himself from the dead. He willingly surrendered His life on the cross, and in doing so, He trusted the Father to resurrect Him. This is what Jesus meant when He cried out, just prior to His death, *"Father, into your hands I commit my spirit"* (Luke 23:46). These words echo David's declaration of his trust in God's saving power:

Since you are my rock and my fortress, for the sake of your name lead and guide me. Keep me free from the trap that is set for me, for you are my refuge. Into your hands I commit my spirit; deliver me, LORD, my faithful God (Psalm 31:3–5).

Just as David trusted God to save him out of the trap of his enemies, Jesus also trusted His Father to resurrect Him out of the trap of death. The devil had one plan, but God had another. Thus, Jesus laid down His life, trusting the Father to raise Him up again. We too, like Jesus and like David, will find strength and deliverance in the choice to trust in the goodness and power of God. He is for us, and when we live in His abundance and blessing, nothing in this life can overcome us.

3. Correct Focus

Third, to fully walk in the victory Christ has already given us, we must maintain correct focus. Our reality (or our perception of reality) is determined by what we focus on. We could be living in incredible abundance, but if we focus on what we still don't have, we will think we live in lack. Conversely, we could be experiencing many difficulties, but if we focus on the promises of God and His blessings in our lives, we will see ourselves as blessed. The truth, according to the Bible, is that as believers we are blessed. Paul says, *"Praise be to the God and Father of our Lord Jesus Christ, who has blessed us in the heavenly realms with every spiritual blessing in Christ"* (Eph. 1:3). When we say yes to Jesus, we receive every spiritual blessing in Him. The New Testament is full of statements about the blessings and abundance of life in Christ. But if we do not believe we are blessed, we will keep ourselves from experiencing those blessings, even though they are part of our inheritance in Christ.

It is a matter of what we look at. James talks about this, saying that when we look intently at the perfect law of freedom (which is Christ's new covenant law of love), we will experience the blessing inherent in it:

But whoever looks intently into the perfect law that gives freedom, and continues in it—not forgetting what they have heard, but doing it—they will be blessed in what they do (James 1:25).

What we meditate on will be the reality we experience. *What we focus on we empower.* In other words, what we focus on has our complete attention. If we focus on the difficulty, the problem, the crisis, then we are not focused on Jesus. When this happens, we begin to evaluate our circumstances through the lens of our opinions, experiences, and perceptions. This is the makings of a major disaster. That is why Paul says to focus on the good things of the Kingdom:

> *Finally, brothers and sisters, whatever is true, whatever is noble, whatever is right, whatever is pure, whatever is lovely, whatever is admirable—if anything is excellent or praiseworthy—think about such things* (Philippians 4:8).

The result of this correct focus is, as Paul says in the next verse: *"Whatever you have learned or received or heard from me, or seen in me—put it into practice. And the God of peace will be with you"* (Phil. 4:9). Paul had modeled a life of faith in God, believing in His promises even in difficulty. This is the example he had set for the Philippians, and he encourages them to, like him, access the peace of God already within them by focusing on God's truth. This is what is possible in Christ. This is how we are made to live, as new creation believers.

Yet many of us do not. Instead, like Jesus' disciples in the Garden of Gethsemane, we allow ourselves to wander from the Father's love and respond to crisis in our own strength and wisdom. Jesus had warned His disciples repeatedly about what was coming. And when He went to the Garden to strengthen Himself, He invited them to join Him. In fact, He exhorted them strongly, *"Watch and pray so that you will not fall into temptation. The spirit is willing, but the flesh is weak"* (Matt. 26:41). For whatever reason, they did not pray but instead fell asleep. Because of this, they were caught unprepared, and they responded to the arrest and death of Jesus poorly. They had seen Jesus respond to difficulty by strengthening Himself in the Father's love. But they had not built their own personal history with the Father, and when they faced their own crisis, they scattered. They empowered fear and doubt in their lives, and as a result, they missed out on the peace of God in the midst of the storm.

Thankfully, the Father was patient with them, just as He is with us. It was not long until these same disciples, newly empowered with the Spirit, learned to live in and from the love of Father God. We can, too. The Father is, as we have said already, always with us. He has given us all we need to live a life of godliness (see 2 Pet. 1:3). The Kingdom is already ours. Yet we have a choice about whether or not we will live in the inheritance He has given us. These three keys—intimacy, trust, and correct focus—play a major part in renewing our minds so that we will see as God sees and, as a result, live in our new identity as beloved and victorious children of God. No matter the situation, in Christ we overcome.

Truth Declarations

GOD LONGS TO BLESS ME EVERY DAY!

I have access to every spiritual blessing (see Eph. 1:3).

God is rejoicing over me with singing (see Zeph. 3:17).

God will never stop doing good to me (see Jer. 32:40).

I am my Father's treasured possession (see Exod. 19:5).

God awakens me every morning, speaking to my heart (see Isa. 50:4).

My Father longs to lavish His grace and compassion on me (see Isa. 30:18).

VICTORY IN CHRIST JESUS IS FULLY MINE!

I am an overcomer in all things (see 1 John 5:4).

Since I am in Christ, so are all my circumstances (see John 16:33).

I have been given the mind of Christ to live from His perspective (see 1 Cor. 2:16).

My Father knows my every need, and I trust in His goodness and lavish provision (see Matt. 6:7–8, 31–33).

I am a much loved child in my Father's family. He is working all things for my good. I am never in lack (see Rom. 8:28).

As a new creation believer, I am able to focus on Kingdom solutions while being guided by His peace (see Phil 4:8–9).

Since I am in Christ, my Father is well pleased with me (see Matt. 17:5).

No weapon forged against me will prosper, because Jesus is my shield (see Isa. 54:17; Ps. 84:9, 11 PT).

I live from victory rather than for victory. Through the finished work of Jesus, the enemy has been fully defeated and has no authority over me (see Col. 2:15).

GETTING PERSONAL

1. Are you currently facing a difficulty or challenge in your life? Briefly record it here.

_____

_____

_____

_____

2. In what ways have you tried to handle this situation in your own power or strength?

_____

_____

_____

_____

3. Ask the Father to overshadow you and fill you with His peace, strength, and courage. Ask Him, *"Father, how do You see this situation? What is Your perspective?"*

_____

_____

_____

_____

4. In what areas of your life do you need to agree with God's truth instead of toxic and negative thoughts? In what situations do you need to trust Him more fully?

_____

_____

_____

_____

CHAPTER 5

The Rest of Love

Nicholas Herman, better known as Brother Lawrence, was a Carmelite monk in France in the mid to late 1600s. Before coming to the monastery near Paris, he was a soldier, a footman, a cabinet officer, and then finally, a monk. As a large and clumsy man, he was prone to making messes. At first, his superiors put him to work in the stables, but eventually they moved him to the only job in the monastery he couldn't mess up—washing pots and pans in the kitchen. Here, with God as his only companion, Brother Lawrence discovered the tangible and abiding presence of God.

Brother Lawrence loved God with all his heart, and he decided to attempt to practice dialoguing with the Lord in his daily activities all day long. After years of practice, his life was so positively transformed and his friendship with God was so recognizable to those around him that a high-ranking church leader sought out Brother Lawrence to be his spiritual advisor. They shared four conversations, and Nicholas wrote him sixteen letters that contained his insights into living in the manifest presence of God.

Simply put, Brother Lawrence had discovered that the way to sense God's presence all day was to have lots of conversations with Him. His goal was to form the habit of talking and listening to Him all the time. The key was continually loving God and recognizing Him as intimately present, as *Immanuel*, which means "God with us." Brother Lawrence learned to set God always before him, to train his mind to continually turn toward Him. He was about his Father's heart and business. After his death in 1692, a collection of those letters on the subject of the contemplative lifestyle were published under the title, *The Practice of the Presence of God*. That little volume has become one of the bestselling Christian books of all time.

The essence of Brother Lawrence's book is how to become friends with God, how to develop a deep and ongoing conversational lifestyle with Him. Our relationships can be organized into five stages, based on their intimacy. Every relationship begins as a casual one, and some progress to deeper levels of intimacy.

Stage 1: **Casual**—I speak as an acquaintance (safe but shallow talk)

Stage 2: **Beginning Trust**—I speak of what I think and feel

Stage 3: **Deep Trust**—I share my dreams, frustrations, mistakes, and fears

Stage 4: **Intimacy**—I sit quietly with my friend, experiencing a presence beyond words

Stage 5: **Union**—I become like that person, speaking, feeling, and acting with his reactions

The same is true in our relationship with God. As children of God, we are all equally loved, yet we do not all experience the same depth of intimacy with God. This is because God offers the depths of relationship with Him to all of us, but our level of intimacy with Him is up to us. We get to choose. This is why it's important to spend time with God.

In Luke 2, when Jesus was just 12 years old, He traveled to Jerusalem with his parents and their relatives and friends for the annual Passover Feast. After the festivities were over, they set out for home. However, on the second day, they discovered that Jesus was not actually with them. So they returned to Jerusalem and found Him in the temple courts, sitting among the religious teachers, listening and asking questions. When His parents found him, they asked why He had stayed behind, giving them all a fright. Jesus' answer shows us, even from a young age, the priority of His focus. *"Didn't you know I had to be in my Father's house?"* (Luke 2:49). In other words, Jesus was saying, "My focus and objective, the core of who I am, is My Father and His business." We too can develop this kind of focus and intentionality in our relationship with our Father. We simply need to practice His presence. Like Jesus, we need to make conversation with the Father our *way of life*, not just a discipline.

Many people are hungry for God, hungry to experience a deep, intimate, and ongoing awareness of the love of the Father. This is the purpose and result of conversation with Him. When practiced consistently, speaking directly with Him and actively listening to His voice leads to a connected relational lifestyle. In other words, practicing two-way conversation with God will eventually enable us to live with an awareness of God's presence and love with us, even in the midst of the busyness of everyday life. Of course, God is with us all the time, whether we are aware of Him or not. He lives within every believer. However, practicing awareness of His presence at all times enables us to live out the abundant new covenant life He has given us.

This may seem weird or impossible to those who have not experienced it, but it is both simple and possible. When we received new life in Christ, He restored our relationship with the Father, and we now have access to Him at all times. His Spirit lives within us, and we have the mind of Christ (see Rom. 8:9–11; 1 Cor. 2:16). Further, as a good Father, He is always thinking about us and speaking to us. All we need to do to encounter God's love is to be still and look at Him. It really is that simple. When we do this regularly, we begin to live a lifestyle of connection with our Father. We begin to continually experience His presence — living under the influence and in the overflow of His love for us. This is not something reserved for the super-holy; it should be the reality for every believer.

INCREASED CAPACITY

All of this comes back to capacity. Once again, Jesus is the example for us. After His excursion in the Temple as a twelve-year-old, Jesus returned to His home in Nazareth with His parents and was obedient to them. There, over the next eighteen years, Jesus grew in wisdom and stature and in favor with God and people (see Luke 2:51–52). After the brief scene in the temple courts, the Bible does not tell us anything more about Jesus until He was ready to start His public ministry at the age of thirty. All we know is that He was maturing physically and spiritually. Mark 6:3 does tell us that Jesus was a carpenter by trade. In that day, it was customary for the sons to learn the father's trade and carry on the family business. While Jesus was growing up, Joseph must have taught him carpentry. All the while, Jesus was also growing in His capacity for relationship with Father God and receiving clearer focus concerning His Father's business.

If Jesus, the perfect, incarnate Son of God had to grow in His spiritual capacity, so do we. The word *capacity* can be defined as "size or volume, ability, or role." For our purposes here, we will concentrate on capacity as ability—the mental or physical ability for something or to do something. We could also refer to this as our capability, aptitude, competence, power, gifting, scope, potential, resources, expertise, and influence. We all build capacity for one thing or another, for good or bad.

For instance, my daughter and her husband are athletes who compete in marathons, iron man competitions, and the like. To do this successfully, they carefully develop and follow a plan for training. This plan is specifically designed to increase their physical capacity and endurance so they will perform well in upcoming events. It also helps them increase their mental capacity so they can stay focused and endure, even when they don't feel like it. The plan is a regular reminder of their objectives. By following it, they are able to build the capacity needed to stay on track and the focus needed to accomplish their goals. Of course, while working the plan, they are faced with choices along the way that will either help or hinder their progress.

On the other hand, we can also build capacity for things that are destructive for us and those around us. This usually happens subtly. It happens when we take our focus from Christ. We start out thinking, *This won't hurt me; I'll be in control; I'll turn this on and off as I want to; I'll walk away when I'm ready.* This is the onramp to addiction. Over time, we build mental, physical, and spiritual capacity for sin. The result is bondage, oppression, and misery. This is the opposite of God's intention for our lives. It is a perversion of the spiritual identity He has given us and our call to increase in favor with God, just as Jesus did.

We need to be intentional about building our spiritual capacity. My daughter and son-in-law are intentional about building their capacity as athletes. They recognize the potential of their bodies, and they find joy in increasing their capacity to perform at greater and greater levels. Our physical bodies are made to be strong and active and able to accomplish great feats. They thrive when we regularly exercise and push our bodies to new limits. Even though it is difficult, it is good for us, and it brings a greater quality of life. Likewise, our spirits are created to exist in union with Father God. In Christ, we are *"filled to the measure of all the fullness of God"* (Eph. 3:19). We are made to live in this reality, which is a gift from God to us. Whether or not we embrace and live in that reality is up to us. It is a question of building and maximizing our capacity to live in our new creation identity.

The question is: *What are we building a greater capacity for in our lives?* Whether intentionally or unintentionally, by the decisions we make, we are increasing our capacity for some things and decreasing it for others. This happens through practice, or what activities we give our time to. The bottom line is, we make time for what is important to us. A lack of time is not an excuse, because when something is really important to us, we find time for it. If we find ourselves saying, "I want to do that, but I don't have time," the issue is not one of time but of priority.

Because of this, it is vital that we deliberately build our spiritual capacity by spending time with our Father. To that end, in this final chapter, we will examine several simple keys to cultivating this intentional lifestyle of staying connected to His love and voice.

BE STILL

The first key a lifestyle of conversation with God is learning to *be* instead of *do*. *Doing* and *being* are two very different things. Simply put, *doing* encompasses all we do for God, things like attending a small group, volunteering, reaching out in the community, serving on committees, and the like. It can even include Bible-reading, church attendance, and prayer—if we are doing these things without a heart connection to the Father. In other words, *doing* is anything we do that does not develop intimacy with God. By contrast, *being* is learning to be still before God and spend time with Him. This is how we cultivate real relationship. We communicate, spending time with Him, listening to Him, and resting in His presence. This is how intimacy is built—in human relationships and in our relationship with God. Through learning to *be* in our relationship with Him, we discover peace, rest, and confidence in Him.

This is a central part of our faith, yet the sad fact is that many Christians do not know how to connect to the Father's heart or recognize His presence. Often, this is simply because they have not been taught about the presence of God. They see Him as their Lord and Savior, but they don't realize He's also their Father and friend. For others, the issue is feeling uncomfortable, like Peter did when God's presence tangibly showed up on the mount of transfiguration (see Matt. 17). Instead of listening and discerning what was happening, he became really nervous and started talking. He didn't know how to *abide* in the Father's presence, so he wanted to get busy *doing* something. While this might be a natural response when we are not used to supernatural experiences, God invites us to set aside our insecurities and to simply be with Him.

Several years ago, I attended a conference on how to hear the voice of the Lord. There I learned two life-changing skills—how to have a conversation with God and how to soak in His presence. Both of these are part of learning to *be*. At the conference, I learned four simple steps to dialoging with God, based on Habakkuk 2:1–2.

1. Become still and quiet in my thoughts and emotions.

2. Fix my eyes on Jesus. Use vision like King David did by picturing Jesus (see Ps. 16:8; Acts 2:25).

3. Recognize His voice as spontaneous flowing thoughts.

4. Write down the flow of spontaneous thoughts which come to me while my eyes are fixed on Jesus.

Using this simple pattern, we can connect to God's heart and learn to hear His voice in response to our thoughts and questions. At first, it may feel difficult to know whether we are hearing God's voice or not. That is normal, because we are just beginning to train our spiritual senses to hear from God. The most common way for God to speak is through a still small voice, which is the voice we hear in our hearts. It wells up from within us.

Of course, it is important to always test what we hear against the Word of God. God will never contradict the Bible. And He also always speaks for the purpose of encouraging, strengthening, and comforting. His voice is never accusing, destructive, or condemning. Even if He is convicting us of sin, He does it in a loving and hopeful manner. He tells us who He made us to be in Him, and that never involves condemnation or fear. God has many wonderful things to say to us. He is always speaking to us. We just need to develop our spiritual senses in order to discern His voice.[5]

The second skill I learned, which has since become one of my favorite activities, is soaking prayer. In a nutshell, this is practicing Psalm 46:10, which says, *"Be still, and know that I am God."* To be still means to "cease from something, to cease striving, to relax, to become quiet." Of course, stillness is not the goal; it is the vehicle for the goal—which is knowing God. We become still in our minds and bodies so that we can know and sense Immanuel with us. The word *know* in Psalm 46:10 means "to learn to know, to perceive, to be made known." It means knowing someone *relationally* and *experientially*. This is the goal in our intimate human relationships, and it should also be the goal in our relationship with God. We do not seek to simply know about Him but to know Him with our hearts.

That is His invitation to us. As our Father, He does not just want to know about us (which He does), but He wants to have personal

---

[5] For more on hearing God's voice, I recommend *4 Keys to Hearing God's Voice* by Mark Virkler.

relationship with us. Thus, He invites us, saying, "Stop what you're doing, relax, and come into My presence so you can know Me personally, relationally, and experientially." By becoming quiet (not talking, praying, or doing anything) and totally focusing on Him, we are able to listen, enjoy, and *be* with Him. As we commune with Him, He gives us fresh revelations of His love and power in our lives.

In our activity-driven culture, being still and quiet is a learned art. It's not something most of us do naturally. In fact, many people have a hard time being alone or sitting in silence. In our modern world, we rarely need to be silent. We have television and music, not to mention the constant stream of media available through our smart phones and tablets. But if we want to learn to know the Father, we need to choose silence and stillness. We need to silence our devices and make ourselves unavailable to anyone but Him. We also need to learn how to quiet our thoughts and emotions.

My favorite way to soak is by using the music of Julie True.[6] She is incredibly gifted to facilitate an encounter in the presence of Father God, Jesus, and Holy Spirit. Simply put on the music, get in a comfortable position on the floor or in a big comfy chair, fix your eyes on Him, and simply receive. Receive His love. Receive healing. Receive from His heart to yours. There you will find rest, love, and joy! Many of us live in a constant swirl of thoughts and emotions. Only when we remove both outer and inner distractions will we be able to learn to recognize the inner voice of the Holy Spirit.

I like to describe soaking prayer as being a lot like the pickling process. To make a pickle, one takes a cucumber and soaks it in a mixture of vinegar and spices for a period of time. During the soaking process, the cucumber is changed superbly into a pickle. Soaking in the Lord's presence is similar to that. As believers, we

---

[6] JulieTrue.com

already have the Spirit of God living within us. Yet if we are unaware of His presence, we inhibit His ability to affect change in our lives. *Soaking* involves making ourselves aware of our union with Christ and His presence within us. As we commune with Him, focusing our thoughts and affections on Him, we are changed progressively into His image.[7]

LOOK TO JESUS

Focusing on Jesus is the second key to a lifestyle of conversation with God. It goes hand-in-hand with learning to *be*. As we sit in silence with the Father, the goal is not to empty our minds completely but to fill our minds with nothing but Him. This is where focus comes in. Many people exercise little control over their thought lives. They may even think they cannot control what comes into their minds. However, the Bible is full of admonitions to steer our thoughts toward God and the good things of His Kingdom. As Paul says, we must *"demolish arguments and every pretension that sets itself up against the knowledge of God, and we take captive every thought to make it obedient to Christ"* (2 Cor. 10:5).

Throughout the Gospels, Jesus taught on the importance of what we choose to set our hearts, minds, and desires on. He said that the object of our attention has a huge impact on our day-to-day living, either for good or bad. In everything He did and said, Jesus showed what it looks like to have a mind continually set toward the Father's heart. Jesus, the Spirit-filled man, was continually under the influence of the Father's tangible presence. One day, when asked why He healed a man on the Sabbath, Jesus answered:

Very truly I tell you, the Son can do nothing by himself; he can do only what he sees his Father doing, because whatever

---

[7] For more on this, see http://vikkiwaters.com/2015/10/14/connecting-with-the-holy-spirit/.

the Father does the Son also does. For the Father loves the Son and shows him all he does. Yes, and he will show him even greater works than these, so that you will be amazed (John 5:19–20).

Jesus only did what He *saw* the Father doing and *heard* Him saying while *in* His presence (see John 8:38). This is the proper place for *doing* in the believer's life. It should always flow from our heart connection with the Father. Continually connecting with the Father was the foundation of Jesus' life and ministry. For this reason, when He approached the end of His life, He emphasized to His followers the importance of staying connected to the Father through the Spirit of God who would live in them (see John 14–16). The apostle Paul also emphasized the need to focus our thoughts on Jesus

Since, then, you have been raised with Christ, set your hearts on things above, where Christ is, seated at the right hand of God. Set your minds on things above, not on earthly things. For you died, and your life is now hidden with Christ in God (Colossians 3:1–3).

Because of who we are—God's beloved children—we should align our thoughts with our actual position in Christ. We should live from His heavenly reality, not what we can see in the world around us. The writer of Hebrews called this *"fixing our eyes on Jesus, the pioneer and perfecter of faith"* (Heb. 12:2). The phrase *"fixing our eyes"* implies looking away from one thing in order to see something else. This is the essence of contemplation. We look away from the outward distractions of the world and the inward distractions of our thought lives, and we turn our focus completely on Jesus. When we do this, we can enjoy simply *being* in His presence, and we can also meditate on His truth and the essence of who He is.

MEDITATE ON TRUTH

The third key to this lifestyle of conversation with God is regularly meditating on God's truth. Christian meditation, or contemplation, is always focused on the three persons of the Trinity or on Scripture (see Josh. 1:8; Ps. 77:12; 119:15). We can meditate on an attribute of God (such as His goodness) or on His works. We can meditate on the life of Jesus or His resurrection power. We can meditate on the creative power of the Spirit or His wisdom. The subjects we could meditate on are limited only by the vastness of the Godhead. No matter what aspect of Him we chose to fix our eyes on, the goal is always the same: to simply be still before the Lord, wait for Him, think about Him, and experience His presence in deep and profound ways. The goal is to position ourselves for a greater revelation of God's presence and love in our lives. Contemplation is the instrument the Spirit uses to bring about our most intimate encounters with God, and as a result, it is transformational.

The secret to successful contemplation is to speak less and listen more. This is another aspect of *being*. We must not fear the silence, but leave lots of room for the Spirit to speak. Following are a few of my favorite truths to meditate on:

1. The King and His Kingdom live within us.

In Luke 17:21, Jesus assured us that the very Kingdom of God is actually *within* our hearts and surrounding us at all times. Because of our relationship with Jesus, we have access to the Father at all times. He is so close. In fact, His Spirit lives within us. Psalm 139:7 tells us God is always with us. It is actually impossible to escape His presence. Even when we feel like He is not close by, the truth is He is. As we chose to agree with that truth, even when we don't feel it, we will become increasingly able to recognize His presence.

2. Father God's will is for us to know Him personally.

In John 17, Jesus prays a tremendous prayer for His disciples and for all who would one day believe in Him. As part of that, He prays:

> Now this is eternal life: that they know you, the only true God, and Jesus Christ, whom you have sent (John 17:3).

In this verse Jesus declares that it is the Father's will for every believer in Christ to *know* the Father as the only true God. In fact, Jesus says that this knowledge actually equates to eternal life. Eternal life, then, is within us *now*, not just when we go to Heaven. In other words, it's not just our destination after death; it is also our quality of life here and now. This is why Paul wrote to Timothy encouraging him to take hold of eternal life. *"Fight the good fight of the faith. Take hold of the eternal life to which you were called when you made your good confession in the presence of many witnesses"* (1 Tim. 6:12). Timothy was already a believer. He was already destined for Heaven. Yet Paul told him that part of fighting the good fight in this life is accessing and walking in the eternal life he had already received. This was not just true for Timothy; it is true for all of us.

3. Father God loves us as much as He loves Jesus.

In another part of His John 17 prayer, Jesus says that God loves us as much as He loves Jesus:

> I am in them and You are in Me. May they experience such perfect unity that the world will know that You sent Me and that You love them as much as You love Me (John 17:23 NLT).

Here, Jesus prays that we would personally know—with our hearts, not our heads—that Father God loves us as much as He loves Jesus. The Father's love for the Son, within the Trinity, is eternal and immeasurable. The crazy and amazing truth is that His love for us is of equal strength and endurance. To help me get this truth into my heart, I have written my first name over the words *them* and *they* in this verse. We could meditate on this reality for all of eternity and still never plumb the depths of His love for us!

4. We are the traveling tabernacle of God.

Psalm 48:9 says, *"Within your temple, O God, we meditate on your unfailing love."* In Moses' time, the tabernacle was a portable structure that represented the place of God's presence. When the Israelites moved from place to place, they would take down the tabernacle and set it back up wherever they settled. Years later, King Solomon built a permanent building called the Temple in Jerusalem. Both were physical buildings where the people of God went to mediate and pray. Both foreshadowed what was to come. In the new covenant, the temple of God is the heart of every believer (see 1 Cor. 6:19). The place where we practice contemplation of our Father's unfailing love is always with us. It takes place in our hearts.

As we practice these three keys to a lifestyle of conversation with God —learning to *be*, looking to Jesus, and meditating on truth—we are building a foundation in our lives. This foundation enables us to eventually begin to live a lifestyle of intimacy with God like Brother Lawrence did. It enables us to go about our daily activities continually aware of God's presence with us and in us. And it enables us to consistently live our lives based on our new covenant reality as His beloved and empowered children.

THE RESULT: REST

The result of a lifestyle of communion and conversation with God is rest. Before I realized who I am as a beloved daughter, I had no idea about rest. My mind was constantly filled with thoughts about what I needed to do. I lived in overdrive, and the idea of rest seemed unattainable. In fact, I believed that if I was not continually getting things done I was goofing off and wasting my time. When Richard and I first married, my inability to rest caused me to feel irritated and uncomfortable when he rested. On Sunday afternoons, Richard loved to nap on the couch while watching sports. To me, this was a sign of laziness, and I did not like it. So, week after week, when he fell asleep, I'd get out the vacuum cleaner and begin my cleaning in the room he was sleeping in. I figured if I needed to work continually, he did too. This, of course, did not go over well. Thankfully, I now realize that I do not need to prove myself or earn anything through hard work. Instead, I have been given the rest of God.

The rest God gives us mirrors His own rest. As the author of Hebrews wrote: *"There remains, then, a Sabbath-rest for the people of God; for anyone who enters God's rest also rests from their works, just as God did from his"* (Heb. 4:9–10). Resting from our works is a spiritual position. It does not mean we never do anything again. Certainly, God has continued to act since His initial creation acts, and He invites us to reign with Him in this life (see Rom. 5:17). The New Testament is full of admonitions to work and labor for God, like this one to the Corinthians: *"Always give yourselves fully to the work of the Lord, because you know that your labor in the Lord is not in vain"* (1 Cor. 15:58). It is not work itself that is bad. It is important. What is bad is work done by orphan-hearted people.

See, as we discussed in chapter 1, orphans work to gain approval, while heirs work because of love for the Father. Thus, the rest we inherit in Christ is the rest of knowing that we belong and are eternally accepted. It is a rest from seeking to be good enough.

In other words, this spiritual rest has to do with our heart attitude, with our position before God. When we know who we are in Him and have stopped laboring for His love, we are able to labor for the Kingdom from a place of rest. And we are able to stop working, without feeling guilty, when we need a break. We are able to relax and enjoy life, knowing that this, too, is part of our inheritance as children of God.

God works because of love, not obligation, and it is this reality that He invites us into when He calls us co-heirs and rulers with Christ. Paul describes exactly this quality in the believers in Thessalonica: *"We remember before our God and Father your work produced by faith, your labor prompted by love, and your endurance inspired by hope in our Lord Jesus Christ"* (1 Thess. 1:3). Their hard work and labor for the Kingdom were rooted in faith, love, and hope. They were not performing to earn God's love but performing because of God's love springing up in their hearts. The distinction may seem small, but it makes all the difference in our ability to live at rest, no matter how full our lives might be.

In God's presence we find the peace we need to stop striving. We find the ability to let go, to trust God, and to simply be with Him. With Him, we discover the rest, refreshment, and renewal we need to be active partners in the expansion of His Kingdom on earth.

The presence of God gives us rest.

In Exodus 33, Moses went to the tent of meeting to experience the presence and glory of God. There God met with him *"face to face, as a man speaks to a friend"* (Exod. 33:11), and He promised him, *"My Presence will go with you, and I will give you rest"* (Exod. 33:14). In this we see a pattern that has continued to our present day. The place of connection with God is the place of rest. And as stated before, true rest means having a heart of rest at all times and in all circumstances. This is what Jesus meant when He said:

Come to Me, all you who are weary and burdened, and I will give you rest. Take My yoke upon you and learn from Me, for I am gentle and humble in heart, and you will find rest for your souls. For My yoke is easy and My burden is light (Matthew 11:28–30).

Here, He was not promising an absence of difficulties or activity in life. He was promising that regardless of what is going on, we can have a heart of rest when our hearts are connected to Him. The more we turn our hearts and attention to Him, the more we will learn from Him, grow in His ways, linger in His presence, and find rest for our souls. This is our inheritance in Christ.

The presence of God gives us refreshment.

One aspect of rest is refreshment, which we also find in God's presence. When I spend time connecting with God, heart-to-heart, peace fills my being. Everything within me feels synchronized with His heart and with Heaven. It is as if my body, soul, and spirit collectively sigh, "Aahhh!" It is like the feeling of drinking a cold glass of water on a very hot day. I am immediately refreshed.

In Acts 3, during Peter's first sermon, as he declared the gospel to Jerusalem on the day of Pentecost, he said: *"Repent, then, and turn to God, so that your sins may be wiped out, that times of refreshing may come from the Lord"* (Acts 3:19). In other words, times of refreshing are part of the gospel message. Refreshment is the result of the inner rest we find in Christ. This happens when we receive Christ into our hearts, and it happens continually as we cultivate our relationship with Him. Because we no longer need to strive for love, but are filled up and overflowing with the love of Father God, we are refreshed. We have renewed energy and vigor.

The presence of God gives us renewal.

Another aspect of rest is renewal. As we rest in His presence, our strength is renewed. We are changed and made new in His presence. When we abide in Christ, we live in constant renewal. Paul says it this way: *"Though outwardly we are wasting away, yet inwardly we are being renewed day by day"* (2 Cor. 4:16). Our physical bodies are aging. They are like jars of clay, which are fragile, easily damaged, and temporary. However, contained within these jars of clay are priceless treasures—our spirits, which are being renewed in Christ. This is our daily reality in Christ. No matter what is going on around us, even when we feel as though we are wasting away, in God's presence we are renewed and strengthened. He gives us all we need.

Communion with God is the foundation of our new covenant lives. In His presence we discover who we are in Him, and we find the rest, refreshment, and renewal we need on a daily basis. In Him we find the answers for our thirst. Jesus promises: *"Let anyone who is thirsty come to me and drink. Whoever believes in me, as Scripture has said, rivers of living water will flow from within them"* (John 7:37–38). In the Kingdom, a drink becomes a stream, and as we receive, we overflow to the world around us.

OVERFLOWING REST

When we intentionally cultivate the presence of God in our lives, the rest in our lives will overflow onto others. The disciples experienced this early on in their witness for Christ. When Peter and John were arrested, the Jewish leaders were astonished at their bravery. The peace that filled their lives, even when they faced persecution, was a witness of the transforming power of Christ. The Bible says, *"They took note that these men had been with Jesus"* (Acts 4:13). These simple and uneducated men were living in their new creation identity because of the transforming power of God's love in their hearts. By spending time with their Father, they were transformed more and more into His image.

This is the benefit of the lifestyle of conversation with God. As Brother Lawrence modeled, all it takes is a desire, commitment to the goal, and the choice to practice. Regularly coming face-to-face with God causes us to be *"transfigured much like the Messiah, our lives gradually becoming brighter and more beautiful as God enters our lives and we become like Him"* (2 Cor. 3:18 AMP). As we live our lives from the place of inner rest, people around us notice. They will be amazed at the anointing we carry. They will recognize that we have been with Jesus.

I have seen this in my own life. When I live my day from a place of rest and peace, with a smile on my face, others are drawn to me. About a month ago, the cashier at my local grocery story told me I was the happiest customer she had ever encountered. I wasn't doing anything special or intentional. I was just living my life as a beloved daughter of God, and she was attracted to Jesus in me. Recently, this same cashier approached me at the store and asked if she could give me hug, and as she did, she complimented me. When I asked God what was going on, He said this woman has a gift of encouraging others, and when she is around the Kingdom in me, she is comfortable operating in her gift.

This is what should happen as we, carriers of the Father's love, go out into the world. Like Jesus, Peter, John, Paul, and Brother Lawrence, we can live from our Father's presence. We can live as new creations, seated with Christ in heavenly places (see Eph. 2:6). We can live in the rest of love.

Truth Declarations

I CAN REST IN MY FATHER'S LOVE.

Jesus, the person of rest, has taken up residence on the inside of me (see Exod. 33:14).

No matter what's going on in my life, I can be at peace and rest as I turn to Him (see Matt. 11:28–30).

Holy Spirit will teach me how to relax and be still in His presence so that I may intimately commune with Him (see Ps. 46:10).

The same Spirit that raised Jesus to life delights to live fully in me (see Rom. 8:9–11).

God has given me the gift of living fully connected to His love for me. I choose to rest in my new creation identity (see Eph. 3:10).

I was created to fix my eyes on Jesus and hear His voice clearly (see Rom. 12:2; John 10:4, 16, 26–27).

I rest in the truth that I have the gift of eternal life to enjoy this side of Heaven (see 1 Tim. 6:12).

Father God loves me as much as He loves Jesus (see John 17:23).

I HAVE A CONFIDENT CONNECTION WITH HIM.

I am made new in His presence every day (see 2 Cor. 4:16).

When my focus is on Him, my Father reveals where He is at work so that I can partner with Him to bring Heaven to earth (see John 5:19–20).

As I commune with Him, I look just like Jesus. Others are drawn to Jesus in me (see Acts 4:13; 2 Cor. 3:18).

Since I am in Christ, I can see and hear what is on my Father's heart (see John 8:38).

Since I have been raised to newness of life in Christ, I choose to align my thoughts to Heaven's reality (see Col. 3:1–3).

I am connected to His presence at all times; He is always with me (see Luke 17:21; Ps. 139:7).

It is my Father's will and desire for me to personally know Him (see John 17:3).

In the new covenant, I am a traveling tabernacle of the presence of God. His unfailing love fills my life (see 1 Cor. 6:19; Ps. 48:9).

I thank God every day that His wrap-around presence, His invisible arms of love, are always open, and I choose to rest in His embrace (see Ps. 84:9, 11 PT).

GETTING PERSONAL

1. What have you built a greater capacity for in the last twelve months?

_____

_____

_____

_____

2. Do you lack hunger for God—but wish you had it? Don't beat yourself up. We all experience dry times in our Christian walk. Wanting to want to spend time with Him is a beginning. Ask Jesus to increase your desire to spend time with Him.

_____

_____

_____

_____

3. Which of the five stages of friendship best describes your current relationship with God? Ask God, *"Father, what do You want to say to me concerning our relationship?"* Pour out your heart to Him and listen.

_____

_____

_____

_____

4. Ask the Holy Spirit to lead you to a verse or passage of Scripture that speaks to a need in your life at this time. Sit quietly and humbly before the Lord, quieting your thoughts and emotions. Fix your eyes on Jesus.

Slowly read a small portion of the passage, taking it in fully, allowing individual words and phrases to stand out to you. Consider things like what this passage, verse, phrase, or word teaches about God, His attributes, His love, life in His kingdom, your relationship with Him, etc.

Invite the Holy Spirit to speak to you by asking, *"Holy Spirit, what do You wish to say to me through this Scripture?"* Record what you sense here.

_____

_____

_____

_____

_____

_____

_____

_____

Do not move on until you have a strong sense that you have received everything God has for you in this moment. Take what you have heard and turn it into a prayer back to Him. Thank Him for the insights and revelations. Affirm your love for Him and receive His love for you.

5. Read and meditate on Psalm 46:10. Turn your full attention to the Lord. This is a time to allow the Father to speak to you by simply surrounding you in His presence. Imagine a quiet, peaceful place in the center of your heart where you are only aware of the Father's love and nothing else.

If you find your mind getting distracted, gently bring your focus back to Him. One technique that is helpful when you realize your mind is drifting is to begin to whisper "Father," "Jesus," or "Holy Spirit." Use that soft, gentle whisper as a vehicle to connect yourself back to His quiet presence. Try to maintain this silence before the Lord, relishing His presence, for ten to fifteen minutes.

Conclusion

As I mentioned in the Introduction, Jesus experienced and confidently walked in His Father's love for Him. He is a perfect model for us. We are made to experience God's love in the same way that Jesus did, and as a result, to live as empowered sons and daughters of God.

Not only that, but we are created for excellence and to excel in all we do. We are created to be pursued and to pursue the *more* of God. That hunger in our hearts is a gift from the Father, who loves us as much as He loves Jesus. This truth is a game-changer. In my life, all the years of striving, searching, and performing came to a screeching halt when I realized I am a much loved child of God. Because I am in Christ, my Father looks at me and sees Jesus. And all that is available to Jesus is available to me.

When I decided to believe and trust in these realities, I began to experience His intimate love for me. There was no turning back! From this place of love, I'm learning more and more, every day, how to walk in my identity with confidence and power, discovering what His love is really like. From this place of love, I can overcome in the midst of trials and live from a place of rest and peace.

The same is available to you. As you step into this new season as a much loved son or daughter of God, receive and embrace these powerful, life-changing truths:

- In Jesus, you are fully approved and accepted.

- You no longer need to strive, perform, or operate from an orphan heart and mindset.

- His unseen arms are always reaching toward you, inviting you to experience them and return to them continuously. His love for you knows no limits.

- Every Kingdom blessing and reality is available to you, right now, to enable you to partner with Him in bringing Heaven to earth just as Jesus did.

- You are an overcomer in every area of your life! Jesus made sure of that. In hard and discouraging times, return to Him to live in your identity as more than a conqueror.

- You can rest in a confident connection with Him. It takes practice and begins by stepping into the security of your identity—knowing who you are, what you carry, and whose you are. Truly, you are *loved like Jesus* (see John 17:23).

About Vikki Waters

As the founder of Growing in Grace Ministries, Vikki has deep compassion for the healing and spiritual growth of others. GGM equips the body of Christ for abundant living, lasting freedom, and effective ministry.

In 1997, Vikki left a ten-year career in human resources to pursue God's call on her life for full-time ministry—to declare and demonstrate the incredibly good news that Father God *is* in a good mood and is actively healing the broken hearted, setting captives free, and lavishly releasing His love and favor on all who will receive!

Through her career as a business woman, civic leader, and entrepreneur, Vikki understands the challenges working people face in balancing a healthy Christian lifestyle with godly principles. She is a gifted teacher who will draw you close and hold you there while she encourages and inspires you to live and walk in the abundant life Jesus has for you. She is a woman you will love, as much for her contagious humor and warmth as for her tender heart and unashamed desire to live daily in the presence of the Lord.

Her credentials and experience as a licensed ordained minister, author, hospital chaplain, Bible teacher, ministry trainer, guest teacher at Lee University, and life coach have made her a compelling and effective witness. But it is her heart that will reach you and draw you into God's presence.

Vikki and her husband, Richard, have been married for nearly thirty years and live in Chattanooga, Tennessee. They enjoy spending time with their daughter, Emily, and her husband, Jack.

Stay Connected

	Website	vikkiwaters.com & iggm.org
	Facebook	Vikki Waters
	Twitter	@VikkiWatersGGM
	Instagram	vikkiwatersggm
	Email	watersv@iggm.org

If you were blessed by this study, I would love to hear from you. Additional training, resources, and teachings are also available.

I encourage you to read this book in a small group, Sunday School Class, Bible study, book club, or with a close friend. Engage the Father's heart together and see where He takes those relationships!